ADVANCE PRAISE FOR *SALESHOOD*

• • •

"*SalesHood* is the best sales management book I have ever read. There are so many inspirational sales management ideas and actions you can put to work immediately."

—Brent Chudoba, VP, GM of SurveyMonkey Audience

"The use of *SalesHood* in our curriculum enriches our students' understanding of today's challenging professional selling process."

—Daniel P. Strunk, managing director, Center for Sales Leadership, College of Commerce, DePaul University

"The sales management and productivity insights in *SalesHood* will help CMOs improve the alignment between marketing and sales."

—Corinne Sklar, chief marketing officer, Bluewolf

"Elay's passion to make the world better for sellers and their managers comes through in every page. Practical, impactful, and passionately delivered, this book is a must-read for any sales manager."

—Donal Daly, CEO, The TAS Group; author of *Account Planning in Salesforce*

"*Saleshood* is the gasoline that fuels the sales engine. These are practical, actionable steps to set your sales team up for success."

—Lindsey Armstrong, board advisor, technology investor, and former executive vice president, salesforce.com

"Elay's insightful and provocative thesis centers on empowering sales leaders through a community of peers and shared experiences that leverages the wisdom of crowds. Elay's deep experience in coaching sales leaders and his anecdotal stories weave a rich, valuable tapestry of learnings."

—Dan Dal Degan, president, Ensighten

SALES
H⦿⦿D

HOW **WINNING** SALES MANAGERS
INSPIRE SALES TEAMS TO **SUCCEED**

ELAY COHEN

GREENLEAF
BOOK GROUP PRESS

Published by Greenleaf Book Group Press
Austin, Texas
www.greenleafbookgroup.com

Distributed by Greenleaf Book Group LLC

For ordering information or special discounts for bulk purchases, please contact Greenleaf Book Group LLC at PO Box 91869, Austin, TX 78709, 512.891.6100.

Design and composition by Greenleaf Book Group LLC
Cover design by Greenleaf Book Group LLC
Cover images:
©iStockphoto.com/blackred
©shutterstock.com/iconspro

Publisher's Cataloging-In-Publication Data

Cohen, Elay, 1971-
  Saleshood : how winning sales managers inspire sales teams to succeed / Elay Cohen.—1st ed.
    p. ; cm.
  Issued also as an ebook.
  Includes bibliographical references.
  ISBN: 978-1-62634-049-7
  1. Sales executives. 2. Sales management. 3. Employee motivation. 4. Success in business. I. Title. II. Title: Sales hood

HF5439.5 .C64 2014
658.3/044   2013942068

Part of the Tree Neutral® program, which offsets the number of trees consumed in the production and printing of this book by taking proactive steps, such as planting trees in direct proportion to the number of trees used: www.treeneutral.com

TreeNeutral®

Printed in the United States of America on acid-free paper

14 15 16 17 18 19   10 9 8 7 6 5 4 3 2 1

First Edition

With love and gratitude to Jenn, Jonah, and Tessa.

CONTENTS

PREFACE

Selling is part of my DNA, culture, and heritage. From the very beginning, selling was always a major focus in my life.

There are generations of salespeople in my family stretching across Europe, the Middle East, and North America. My grandfather sold carpets out of a little shop in Cairo, Egypt. My father started out selling sewing machines (in broken English) when he first landed in Canada, and then expanded his specialization to selling all types of furniture in a large retail store. My mother is a real estate professional, always focused on networking and building relationships with new clients. I grew up living, breathing, and witnessing sales. It became an important part of who I am from the very beginning.

Looking back to my early days, starting at age five, I remember my father bringing me to his retail furniture store in Toronto on weekends and in the summer to help. I remember standing at the front door, being coached on what to say as prospective customers walked in the store. Foot traffic was a big source of leads for the business. I would share, with a big smile, the special of the day and invite them in to sit on a sofa. I remember learning about the importance of decision-making processes and relationship building very early on in life, before I even knew that those were concepts sales teams counted on to make money.

Fast-forward ten years: As a young entrepreneur, I was knocking on doors, signing up customers for my new lawn-cutting and landscaping services. Two years later, with a briefcase full of first-aid supply samples, I plotted a route, walking up and down the streets of Toronto's industrial parks, pitching my wares and replenishing as many first-aid boxes as I could. I cherish those early experiences. Selling first-aid supplies taught me a lot about perseverance, making the most of a territory, and the ups and downs of knocking on doors. These early days selling and entrepreneurial experiences continue to serve me well, especially in Silicon Valley. I'm proud to have picked up skills in my childhood that are so foundational: confidence, prospecting, passion, intensity, relationship building, results driven, and entrepreneurialism.

In my twenties, I worked in many sales positions. I worked in sales at one of the largest financial institutions in Canada. I helped customers with their portfolios, selling investment and credit products. I entered the technology space with a couple of close friends as we founded a company called CampBrain, selling automation solutions to children's summer camps. After completing my MBA, I sold Internet services for a company called Mackerel Interactive during a time when we interpreted "WWW" as the "world wide wait." We ended up building the first interactive website for a Canadian bank. I also helped sell consulting and marketing services to some of the largest companies in the world, such as Ford, GM, HP, and IBM, while working at Maritz Canada.

I moved to San Francisco and at Allegis co-created a software category called Partner Relationship Management (PRM), where we offered technology solutions to optimize distribution channels. I then worked in the sales-engineering and industry-business-unit organizations at Oracle, selling CRM and PRM applications. Salesforce.com® was my next stop, where I relaunched PRM.

The PRM product was a tremendous success measured by market share, revenues, and customer success. Besides creating a great product, the success of the product was hugely attributed to the way we powered sales enablement. As customer and sales focused product executives, we rolled up our sleeves, worked with the sales teams on customer deals, offered up sales office hours, and built a strong sense of community around this product, both inside the company and outside, with our own partners.

In 2007, after a successful launch of PRM, a number of huge customer wins, and some innovative sales engagement, I was asked to lead sales productivity at salesforce.com. In my role as senior vice president for sales productivity, we focused on all things "sales enablement," including onboarding, training, events, sales process, sales tools, communications, deal support, coaching, incentive trips, executive programs—such as the briefing center—and much more. Anything and everything that sales teams needed to be more productive came through our productivity group. The team grew from ten people to more than one hundred in 2013. Consider the salesforce.com revenue, customer, and employee growth trajectories between the years 2005 and 2013: it was a rocket ship. We experienced double-digit growth, month after month and year over year.

The sales productivity success is attributed to the leadership and mentorship provided by Frank van Veenendaal, the vice chairman leading all things sales for over a decade. An important lesson from working for Frank was experiencing the power of aligning sales productivity with our go-to-market strategies. We lived in sales and we iterated our programs together with sales leaders. We charted new territory and created a new way to sell subscription software services in a "software as a service" (SAAS) world. We rolled out several transformational initiatives that resulted in unprecedented sales productivity growth. We experienced improvements in customer-facing selling time, pipeline quality, and win rates. We evolved from a single-product company to a multiproduct, multisolutions company. Our creativity and innovation in sales productivity are definitely responsible for a big part of this success.

Global sales productivity was a program machine. We onboarded thousands of salespeople and customer-facing employees. We ran over one hundred sales boot camp programs. We ran thousands of training events, including several sales kickoff events, some of which were in places like Las Vegas and others that were delivered virtually. We created a set of sales values that anchored all of our sales productivity initiatives and deal-based activity. We iterated the sales process and the supporting sales automation technology many times to meet the changing dynamics of the market and the competitive landscape. We executed thousands of deal support requests, helping salespeople improve win rates and grow their deal sizes. We curated the delivery of the content, training, and sales playbooks.

There are several themes that emerge as I reflect on this amazing experience. First, the best and most productive sales teams and salespeople had a shared consciousness, understanding, and intensity of how to sell and how to win. They were united by a shared set of values. They were connected by a culture and common language anchored in creativity, curiosity, and customers.

Second, the best salespeople and sales teams were ready and willing to share their experiences with one another. "Win as a team" and "never lose alone" became mantras rather than rhetoric. The most successful salespeople were open to sharing their deal strategies and winning sales tools with their peers. Communication lines were opened on teams, across teams, and between geographies. Winning and losing sales experiences were shared by salespeople through mentoring, in team meetings, and at global events like sales kickoffs.

Third, the salespeople that were the most successful were the ones that had a hunger to improve their skills. They were ready to invest time in self-development and sales training. They appreciated and respected the need to refresh skills and learn from each other.

As I was writing this book, the word *SalesHood* emerged as a concept that captures the essence of what makes salespeople and sales teams successful. SalesHood came to life when I started thinking about the words *community*, *consciousness*, and *experience* in the context of the sales world. After bouncing between philosophical books, blogs, and Wikipedia, I landed on a term that stuck with me: "selfhood." This means a lot of different things to many different people, but one definition that emerged was "the fully developed self."

I thought, *What would a fully developed sales executive look like? How would a salesperson realize his or her full potential better and faster?* I applied the selfhood principles and definition to the sales world and saw parallels. The way a sales executive actualizes his or her full potential as a winning salesperson is by reaching a state of confidence, competence, and consciousness, both individually and with the team. The social side of salespeople learning from each other is critical to the power of sharing experiences and best practices. After reaching this point, the word *SalesHood* jumped out at me. The amazing part of this story that I still can't believe was that the URL was available, too!

As I thought more about what SalesHood means, I reflected on what sales training and sales management has been like. Decision-making has been very corporate and headquarter-centric rather than local and empowering. Sales teams have been under the gun to comply with sales certification programs rather than be creative and solve problems. Learning events have been the norm with sales kickoffs and weeklong training workshops eating up selling time rather than learning moments and ongoing training. Sales management has been very hierarchical and top down rather than inclusive, fostering a culture of sales team engagement.

The question then became how to scale SalesHood. Technology is a method but not the only answer. It became apparent that the greatest power to help salespeople and sales teams reach their full potential—SalesHood—is with the first-line sales manager. **If you are a first-line sales manager, this book is for you.**

In this book, I propose a way of thinking and acting for sales managers to embrace sales productivity best practices and inspire sales teams to accelerate sales performance. *SalesHood* is collection of stories and experiences of some of the most successful sales managers and sales productivity best practices.

Empowering a shared set of values and sales consciousness across a sales team is the sales manager's job; they are in the driver's seat to inspire their sales teams to achieve great things. By embracing the responsibility that sales managers have as the major contributors to the development of winning sales teams, they become the powerful lever to achieve SalesHood. Inspired by these principles and values, I founded SalesHood with my cofounder Arthur Do.

So, as you read, think of this book as an investment in building winning sales teams. This can become a foundation and playbook for measuring and motivating your salespeople to realize incredible results.

The book has an introduction in chapter 1, followed by two parts. The introduction dives into the importance of enabling sales managers to be true entrepreneurs and CEOs of their businesses. The first part then focuses on investing time and resources in sales managers' most important asset: their team. The second part dives into sales execution and the importance of a sales manager having a proven sales playbook that is embraced by sales teams and appreciated by customers.

Consider this book a prescriptive set of strategies and tactics to be immediately applied to your business. You'll uncover the key levers you can use to drive up sales productivity and grow your business.

CHAPTER 1

EMPOWER LEADERSHIP

Who would have thought that a simple breakfast meeting with a group of sales managers would be one of the most important events of my professional career? I certainly didn't expect it when I arranged for the group of us to get together. We met at a diner in San Francisco called Rocco's sometime after I'd left salesforce.com. My goal for the meeting was to share some sales productivity ideas I was investigating as a business and to hear their views.

We talked a lot about what was great in their sales management professional lives, and then we shifted to what could be improved. Given my experience and focus, I was especially curious about what would make these sales managers even more productive. What they shared with me that morning ultimately led to an evolution in the way I started to rethink sales productivity and the vital role of first-line sales managers.

The sales managers shared with me the tension they see. On the one hand, corporations have a company business plan informed by company priorities. These priorities are important to the company's success and appreciated by sales managers as they look for guidance on how to run their franchises. On the other hand, the sales manager has a unique team of quota-carrying salespeople, and that team's needs differ from those of other teams in the company. The first-line sales manager is the one with the feet on the street, the one who can best gauge the needs of the team. Sales managers see the important nuances of their territory, their team's strengths and weaknesses, and the product they're selling. These unique, local, and sometimes geographical needs can become lost in the context of broad company priorities.

Don't get me wrong: I'm not saying that the CEO of a company should not have a core set of business goals that are communicated and adopted by everyone in the company. What I am saying is that first-line sales managers need to operate under the construct of the company's business goals while also acting like CEOs in their own right, personalizing their unique go-to-market strategies to their realities. These sales managers must be truly empowered to affect all areas of the business, including but not limited to hiring, marketing, and training.

During the breakfast meeting, the sales managers talked about their marketing programs and training initiatives, saying that they wished they could create even more personalization for their markets and teams. On the marketing side, they wanted to execute city-specific and even customer-specific marketing programs. They also wished to personalize their sales training needs to fit the needs of their sales teams. And they told me bluntly that this type of empowerment would help them drive up their business, growing more pipeline and accelerating sales performance.

One sales executive who was there summed up the group's feelings well. "I've got ten salespeople," she told me. "Each one of them has a different set of skills and experiences. As the sales manager, I need to have a plan for my team and for each and every individual salesperson. The training programs the company gives me are great, but I need to be able to personalize them for my people and deliver them at precisely the right time. Same goes not just for training, but for sales support, marketing programs, and team events."

These sales managers were telling me they wanted to be able to lead their teams in an empowered, personalized way. All of a sudden, my eyes were open to this new reality: Sales managers are looking for ways to better impact their salespeople and their customers with their personal touch. Isn't every salesperson different and every customer scenario unique, too? Sales managers and their teams are at the pulse of what the customer needs. They have the local relationships, and they drive the innovation, marketing, and education on behalf of the company. They are the evangelists— they do a lot of the work. They need to be able to apply resources to their customers and deals in real time. I realized that, given the incredible technology available to any company today, this vision of the empowered sales manager was more attainable than ever. Now, the journey to realize this empowered state begins by transforming thinking and action across the sales manager community and corporations.

After that meeting, I was on a quest. I then talked to hundreds of sales managers about this developing idea and grew increasingly excited as it resonated with person after person. In my talks with sales managers I began to hear many examples of those who were taking action into their own hands, though they were remaining under the radar. For example, one sales manager told me that he couldn't get a demonstration video approved by marketing, so he hired a local video-production shop to create one that would wow his customer and accelerate his sales cycle. Another sales manager shared about hiring sales coaches for her team, paying for it out of her own pocket.

The growth of sales manager empowerment is there and ready to be tapped into; sales teams are ready to be inspired to do great things.

Many will agree that the most important link in the chain is the first-line sales manager. But what folks don't talk about as much is how to actually enable the first-line sales manager to be a true CEO of his or her business. They don't talk much about how the first-line sales manager needs to run every part of the operation, including planning, motivating, and executing, with budget authority that maps to his or her business contribution. All too often, these functions are relegated to headquarters. As I talked to more and more sales managers, the power of this concept began to cement itself in my head. I knew I was on to something. I was quickly reminded of the many examples of entrepreneurial sales managers I worked with in my professional career. The rise of the importance of the sales manager became a central theme in my work and thinking.

SALES MANAGERS ARE OUR MAYORS

The notion of empowering first-line sales managers began to bubble up simultaneously in other parts of my life, too. At a TED conference I heard a great talk by Benjamin Barber, who spoke convincingly and passionately about the power of mayors in driving educational, economic, and environmental change. He titled his book *If Mayors Ruled the World*.[2] In the world of politics, the mayor is where the proverbial rubber meets the road. As I sat listening to the talk, it struck me: The same was true of first-line sales managers. They were the ones who had the same power to effect real change in business. Are sales managers the mayors of our corporations?

After the conference, I sought out more on the mayor concept. Thomas Friedman had an article entitled "I Want to Be a Mayor" that further highlighted the parallels between mayors and sales managers.[3] And that piece, in turn, introduced me to a book by Bruce Katz and Jennifer Bradley, *The Metropolitan Revolution: How Cities and Metros Are Fixing Our Broken Politics and Fragile Economy*.[4] These authors write about the rise of mayoral power through focus, ownership, and hard work.

Applying these principles to the world of sales makes a lot of sense to me. Many sales managers concurred. One sales leader replied saying, "I love the mayor metaphor." Just as there are mayors who are driving radical educational and economic reforms of their constituents, so too are there sales managers who take ownership of their sales team's destiny. The best first-line sales managers take control of all aspects of their business. For example, they own customer relationships and customer success; they are responsible for pipeline health.

As I continued to reflect, I realized that the best sales managers I worked with at salesforce.com were the ones who took matters into their own hands. They were already leading the way, owning their outcomes like the mayors described by Thomas Friedman. The most successful sales managers were the ones who took ownership of their customer relationships, business planning, and team prioritization. These sales managers asked for budgets or found creative methods, such as leveraging relationships with partners, to fund their own marketing events with customers in order to build demand. These sales managers hosted breakfasts and dinners to keep connections alive and to nourish their local network. As with mayors, successful sales managers know that budgets and funding play a major role in driving successful programs that add value to customers—or, in mayor-speak, the constituents.

But in some corporations, allocating funds to first-line sales managers is not easy. Issues of scale emerge around requests, approvals, and tracking the return on investment. And yet I watched the best of the best avoid fighting the battles with corporate and work directly with their top partners to lead their teams with an empowered, entrepreneurial mind-set. They found the money through partnerships to do the programs that made sense. When sales managers are entrepreneurial in their views of their team and their business, they find themselves creatively solving problems and ultimately creating more pipeline, more revenues, and deeper customer relationships.

DO YOU HAVE A PLAN FOR YOUR BUSINESS?

Over the course of the book, we're going to look at how you can become an empowered, entrepreneurial sales manager and how you can operate like the CEO of your territory as you inspire your sales teams to achieve amazing results. But before we get into part I—where we'll talk about building, training, and inspiring your sales team—we need to talk about one of the fundamentals of empowered sales leadership: planning your year. The very first step to taking accountability for your team is setting a vision for how the year is going to unfold, a plan for how and when you're going to employ all the tools we'll cover in this book.

Picture this: You're a sales manager and it's the first day of a new financial year. You've just finished a great year and your team is celebrating their successes. You're reflecting on your sales team's wins and losses. You're doing your personal team scorecard to see who is going to Hawaii and who is not. The year's ups and downs are still fresh in your mind.

The entrepreneurial sales manager will take this time, if she hasn't done so already, to plan out the next year. She'll look to her corporate leadership team for key themes and priorities that she'll need to support in the upcoming year, but she'll also start thinking about how she can localize and tailor those themes and priorities for her own sales team.

She'll also take inventory of her sales team's strengths and weaknesses so she can be proactive about hiring and recruiting. Are there any members of her sales team who should be thinking of a new career? Does she have the right coverage model in place? She'll consider her industry focus, geographic distribution, and product mix as she looks at the coverage of her franchise.

The entrepreneurial sales manager will take stock of the health of the business. She'll keep key performance indicators—such as pipeline, revenue, win rates, new logos, number of deals per salesperson—top of mind. She'll take responsibility for knowing her business. She'll prioritize these metrics across the realities of her business and set stretch goals that will push her team. Successful sales teams and companies have great alignment across a set of metrics intended to drive actions that move the business. She'll be honest about the gaps that exist in the pipeline and work out a strategy for immediate action in the upcoming year.

Part of planning the year is setting the year's theme. One year at salesforce.com, we needed to dial up sales in an emerging product line; it was a top company priority. We announced the "Year of the Service Cloud" to the entire company. At a local level, all sales managers understood what this meant to them and their sales teams, and they took action. They made it happen. Sales manager plans included revenue and pipeline targets mapped to selling this product line. Individual business plans created by sales managers included demand generation and customer programs focused on building outreach to key buyers of the Salesforce Service Cloud® product line. The metrics were clear and the specific product push was also supported by incentives for salespeople.

If your company hasn't set a clear theme for the year, it's your job as sales manager to step up and create one yourself. Your sales teams will appreciate it; it will guide them and give them focus.

Take a chapter from work performed by Tony Robbins to prepare yourself for the year ahead. Close your eyes. (Insert motivational music of your choice.) Visualize what your sales team will look like at the end of the twelve months. Visualize success for you and every salesperson. Have that picture of the celebratory dinner where everyone is sharing his or her success stories. Think of your customers. Think of the must-win accounts you will close this year. Create a story that will become your future. Write down your story and your goals and share it with your team. Be transparent, and hold yourself accountable to the team for stretch goals.[5]

Have your sales team do a similar exercise. Inspire them to think bigger. By the way, you can apply this practice to your team anytime, not just at the beginning of the year. Have them visualize and write down their goals and stories at the start of each month or quarter.

Following are some questions you can use as you apply these planning and motivational strategies with your teams. I know they work, because I used these questions for a motivational push that was well received by sales leadership. Ask your team to compare their current plan and story with a bigger potential. Personalize these questions to your style and business:

- Will you make your number? **Or will you blow your number out beyond belief?**

- Will you close the pipeline in front of you today? **Or will you hunt, find, and close loads of new pipeline?**

- Will you help customers be successful? **Or will you transform their businesses?**

The questions can go on and on, based on what you're trying to accomplish.

• • •

Are you ready to inspire your team to achieve greatness in their careers? Are you ready to help your sales team exceed their goals and targets? My goal with this book is to provide you with tools to develop a strategy for your business that results in exceeding sales targets by distributing pipeline and revenue success across your entire team. Let's make every one of your salespeople a superstar who achieves amazing results. Empower yourself, and become the CEO of your sales team. It's up to you to help your sales teams reach their full potential. SalesHood is within your reach. As a sales manager, you are where the action happens. When you embrace the tools and philosophies described in the chapters of this book, you'll find that everyone on your team is blowing out his or her numbers each quarter and that the entire team is getting recognition for being crucial to the organization's success.

PART I

THE TEAM

CHAPTER 2

START WITH VALUES

For a team of salespeople to be effective, its members have to share a common set of values. It doesn't matter what you're selling, and it doesn't matter whether you're at a ten-person start-up or a ten-thousand-person corporation—if the group shares a core set of values and is speaking the same language, you will reap great rewards. These shared values are the foundation of everything good in a sales organization, and yet many sales teams have not yet taken the critical steps of establishing them clearly.

When a sales team is aligned—from the frontline salespeople and support staff all the way up to the top executives—great things happen. Team members understand their priorities, thrive on the culture, and understand how and when to engage with customers. Everyone is on message; they know what to say and when to say it.

I saw this firsthand during my time at salesforce.com. The company's CEO, Marc Benioff, is a master at motivating, educating, and aligning the entire company and the global sales teams with the most important strategies, and watching him was truly inspirational.

I fully realized the power of the alignment Marc provided at every internal and external event. I remember one of our clients—the president of a large communications company—saying to me, "I know that everyone at this company is on the same page, because everyone is saying the same thing, but in their own words."

The comment struck me. Salesforce.com employees understood the company's values so well that they could express them in their own way, and our clients noticed it!

As I tell nearly every sales manager I meet during my travels, if you can nurture a set of values from your sales team and get everybody on board with them, the benefits are huge: You get motivated, fulfilled employees; satisfied customers; more sales; and sustainable growth.

But so many companies and sales teams don't invest enough time into building these values, even though it's such an important concept. When I start working with a new company to help ramp up their sales productivity, I start by asking them, "Can you share your sales values with me?" Often the answer comes haltingly. The values are usually there somewhere, but they're buried. They're part of a loose subculture instead of being the very foundation of everything the teams do. They're used on an ad hoc basis instead of as a set of mantras that foster consistency and repetition.

If you want to transform your team, establishing clear sales values is the place to start. The values will become the foundation of your sales team—its culture and its processes. Push your limits in sales leadership and make it a priority. Take the initiative; no one else will. This is your chance to shine!

BELIEVE IT; IT WORKS

I was asked to share some sales productivity insights with a leading technology company. I worked with their head of sales operations, and then I was invited to spend some time with their top executives. I listened to their challenges and learned a lot about their business. It became apparent that nurturing this company's sales values would align their sales teams and accelerate their sales performance. We needed to bring their sales values to life by tapping into the company's best practices for sales. Adopting a strategy of sales values had worked for us at salesforce.com, and I was prescribing a similar strategy here.

I thought the call went well, and the executive team gave us some runway to execute. Two weeks later, after we did the research and documentation and started planning the rollout of the sales values to their teams, I found out that the executive team had been a bit skeptical about creating a foundational set of sales values. I talked with the president and he shared that he'd thought all this talk of values and culture was a bit fluffy, but seeing their values come to life had turned him from a nonbeliever into a believer.

The sales values became the ultimate unifier for this company; they emerged in the company's sales system and sales management reporting. The sales values formed the foundation for new hire onboarding and training, showing up on day one of new-hire boot camp and being reinforced many times during training. The entire sales organization was trained on the sales values, too, including "train the trainer" sessions for the sales managers. The values started emerging in deal conversations and reviews, spreading throughout the entire company. It also became apparent that the sales values were *not* present in deals that were going sideways, but once the sales values were reinforced in these deals, they almost always began to move forward. The CEO of the company also embraced the new sales values and presented them in an all-hands company call where he stressed the importance of these sales values to the future of the company. Forecasting accuracy was improved. In a very short period of time, the sales values had become part of the company's culture, and it made a huge difference in how its sales teams operated. At the end of 2013, the company reported the best year ever in its growth and sales productivity metrics.

VALUES IN ACTION: TWO EXAMPLES

In a recent article in the *New York Times* column "Corner Office," Adam Bryant interviewed the CEO of Hilton Worldwide, Christopher Nassetta. This article discusses leadership and aligning values, culture, and strategy. I was struck by the relevance of this interview to the topic of teams and alignment. In the context of a cultural transformation and corporate alignment, Nassetta explains that he asked his teams at Hilton to boil down their value statements and then held a two-day off-site meeting where all these value statements were consolidated. Nassetta said to them, "Let's use some of our own skills and brand it, not because I want to be cute about it, but because people will remember it." The result was an acronym —HILTON— that collected the company's values:

H for hospitality

I for integrity

L for leadership

T for teamwork

O for ownership

N for now

"To reinforce them," Nassetta says, "we are constantly referring to the letters—in newsletters, in town halls—almost to the point where we are driving people crazy. But it works."

This is a very powerful example of mapping core values to a winning formula that transcends leadership and becomes culture. Every company has a unique word that represents its sales values. Even though the Hilton story is company-wide, the principles apply to a sales organization and even a sales team. While the Hilton executive team spent time together in a two-day off-site, the same sales values can be nurtured in an iterative way with sales best prac-tices, customer interviews, and old-fashioned team brainstorming.

Another example of a great company that developed and branded their sales and service values is Apple. They train their retail sales employees to solve customer problems first and then to sell solutions to their needs. "Apple lays its 'steps of service' out in the acronym APPLE,"[6] writes Yukari Iwatani Kane and Ian Sherr in the *Wall Street Journal*. The acronym is a guide for how to engage with customers:

"**A**pproach customers with a personalized warm welcome,"

"**P**robe politely to understand all the customer's needs,"

"**P**resent a solution for the customer to take home today,"

"**L**isten for and resolve any issues or concerns," and

"**E**nd with a fond farewell and an invitation to return."

These values come to life every time one walks into any Apple store in any city. The staff is amazing and the experience is person-alized and consistent.

Both HILTON and APPLE represent a set of values that come to life in the form of an acronym that is mapped to their culture and is easy for salespeople and employees to remember and embrace in their day-to-day activities.

Creating your own HILTON or APPLE sales formula needs to become a top priority: one of the first steps on your mission to inspire your sales teams to succeed.

SALESFORCE.COM'S SAAS MODEL: SUCCESS

In 2007, Frank van Veenendaal, Jim Steele, Linda Crawford, and I met to discuss the future of sales productivity at Salesforce.com.

The challenge they proposed was: How to create a repeatable winning sales playbook that would be quickly adopted by the entire sales organization? We concluded that a set of sales values nurtured from the "heart and soul" of the sales organization would serve us well. But, it had to come from sales teams themselves in order to be fully adopted. We identified top-performing sales leaders who helped us create the Salesforce.com sales values. As of 2014, these sales values are still being used by sales teams and in sales training.

In his book *Behind the Cloud*, Marc Benioff shares the sales values that Dave Rudnitksy instituted within his own sales team.[7] Here is an excerpt of the highlights:

Think Big, Have Attitude.

No Deal Is Won or Lost Alone.

Connect the Dots Focus on "Why Not?"

Always Take the Deal off the Table.

Get Your Face in the Place.

Fun Facts Build Instant Credibility.

Be Proactive on All Paperwork.

Always Get Quid Pro Quo in Negotiations.

Share Best Practices.

Go After Game Changers.

Like Apple and Hilton, we came up with a memorable acronym, too. We called it SUCCESS. Each letter came to reflect a core value. We worked closely with the corporate and brand marketing teams to come up with the SUCCESS brand. It aligned the sales teams with the best of the best and also gave our executive team a scalable way to influence sales activity and behaviors. These sales values can be used by any organization looking to sell like the way we did at Salesforce.com. The acronym is a great blueprint for embracing key tenets of the new subscription-selling model.

The SUCCESS formula evolved from interviews and a lot of hard, creative work. I encourage you to visit the salesforce.com Dreamforce® YouTube channel to look for presentations titled "How Salesforce Runs Its Business." Listen to sales leaders share what SUCCESS means and how they depend on it every day to keep teams aligned.[8] You can also hear from salespeople themselves, who share how they sell and why this sales formula is critical in helping them exceed their quotas, year after year.

Each letter has meaning and is explained in the following illustration and discussion:

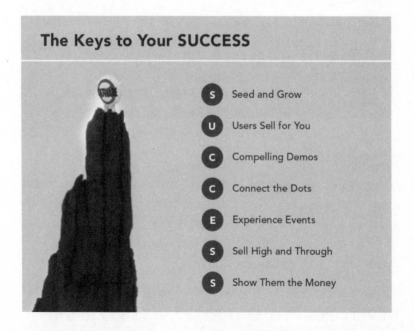

The Keys to Your SUCCESS

- S Seed and Grow
- U Users Sell for You
- C Compelling Demos
- C Connect the Dots
- E Experience Events
- S Sell High and Through
- S Show Them the Money

Seed and Grow: Start small. Build credibility. Build trust. Grow the business.

Users Sell for You: Have customers share their success stories with other customers. Share customer stories early and often in sales cycles.

Compelling Demos: Conduct discovery and uncover buyers' top challenges to create a customized demonstration reflecting company-specific needs.

Connect the Dots: Leverage relationships with key decision makers and influencers. Connect the dots with employees, customers, and partners.

Experience Events: Use events to generate pipeline and improve win rates. Drive more business by using large and small events to drive momentum.

Sell High and Through: It is really important to walk the halls. Look across the entire corporate suite and make sure you understand the top priorities.

Show Them the Money: Focus on the return on investment that customers will realize. Build a specific business case for a customer.

These sales values represent a best practice in subscription selling. The power and impact came to fruition when they were integrated with the culture and cadence of the sales organization. The effectiveness of creating and adopting your own sales values can be that extra push that shifts results from making your numbers to exceeding targets month after month.

DEVELOPING YOUR TEAM'S SALES VALUES

Sales values should come from the heart and soul of an organization. As you set out to build them, you'll need to answer two main questions:

- What are my sales teams doing now that I want to see continue and repeated?

- What needs to change to make our sales teams better?

In other words, the process of building sales values starts by examining what's working and what's not. That way, you can construct a set of values that reinforces the good, sidelines the ineffective or unimportant, and gives everyone a clear set of priorities to follow.

The key to driving sales values across an entire sales organization and making long-lasting impact is to have it start with executives as a top priority. Make it known why your sales executives care about this. Put these people front and center of the messaging and the rollout. Your sales values will acquire more meaning and respect from sales teams. The success of a sales transformation initiative is dependent on the top leaders and sales management enabling the change. Having the right executive support ensures the right level of intensity and helps to make the project a success.

The task of creating a set of values for the sales team is not a single-person job. You, as the sales manager, or top sales leader, can't hand down a list of values to your people and expect them to hop on the train. If you want the team to really engage with the values, you need to give them a role in the process.

Start by assembling a team to do some data collection. These should be people who have the trust of the sales organization. This team will do the interviews and synthesize the data along with the deal stories. If they do not have credibility with the sales organization, the interviewees will not be as open to sharing the truth. Set up a committee and project team to do the interviews and to conduct the surveying, or do it yourself if you can invest the time. Partner with marketing and sales operations to help scale this important due-diligence process. Top salespeople and sales managers across all segments and roles should be interviewed and listened to very closely. Newly hired and struggling salespeople should also be interviewed to counterbalance the views. Don't forget to talk to customers about their buying experience.

After you collate a wealth of feedback, shift into brainstorming mode to prioritize and brand the sales values that fit your culture. Look for words that are at the core of who you are and what you do.

Then turn the words into a sales aid that can be easily distributed. You know you have a winner when your sales value brand or image is pinned up in the desks and cubes of the salespeople because they appreciate it and depend on it.

At company after company, sales values have had a profound impact on sales performance, culture, and revenues. Having an entire sales and customer-facing organization rallied around key selling principles and values results in win-rate improvements, and deal sizes get larger. Deal-review calls and regular sales team meetings become more fun. New hires in sales are onboarded faster and better.

MAKE YOUR SALES VALUES STICK

Once you establish your sales values, the next step is to make them stick. Do not assume that "if you build it, they will come." You will need to fully embrace the sales values and make them a core part of your sales culture. This will take time and executive sponsorship. You will need to have a strategy to integrate them with your sales events, executive communications, sales-manager coaching guides, onboarding programs, technology, and even compensation.

Consider making your sales values a key part of an annual sales kickoff event. At Salesforce.com, when we rolled out SUCCESS we had Frank and Jim (our co-presidents at the time) share their advice and perspectives at our sales kickoff event.Use them as central themes and have your speakers refer to them over and over. Repetition and more repetition is critical to making the values part of your sales DNA. Create a mantra that reaches every person in the sales organization. Have your CEO, sales leaders, top sales executives, and salespeople speak at all the sales events. Use personal anecdotes and deal wins to exemplify why they are so important. Hand them out so your teams can see them. Create posters around the office. Indoctrinate your new hires with this knowledge. Explain each point and use real-life examples to highlight each sales value. You want your entire sales organization to walk away repeating the mantra over and over. Create a mantra that everyone easily remembers, and watch it go viral.

Remember that you—the sales manager—are the most important leverage point for making these kinds of sales productivity programs successful. Without your support and adoption of these values, you won't get the needed reinforcement in the field. It is key that you understand how important this is to the future of your company.

The sales values should also be reinforced using technology and added to your sales process (in chapter 9, we'll talk about the sales process in much more detail.) Create your own specific fields in your sales IT systems. Build workflow rules and email alert triggers that remind salespeople what to do when. For example, a great tool to send salespeople is a listing of questions or common customer objections at relevant stages of the deal, thereby reinforcing the values and adding benefits to the salesperson.

Getting your sales values documented and shared with your sales teams are some of the most important steps in propelling a winning sales culture. Values are what salespeople learn when they are first onboarded and ramped. They support scale and growth in regions around the world. They keep salespeople focused on doing the right things. They inform the sales process. A winning sales team is always aligned by the same end goal of focusing on customer value and customer success. The sales management load is made easy, because managers can rely on the sales values to push alignment, peer coaching, and mentoring. The key to this powerful alignment is to have clear messages that are repeated over and over.

SALES VALUES ARE IMPORTANT FOR BIG AND SMALL BUSINESSES

Building a sales culture and supporting sales values are important for large and small businesses. A friend and colleague, Andrew O'Driscoll, runs a services operation with forty-five-plus employees. We talked about his business and concluded that a sales values exercise would deliver the focus he desired in order to exceed his company goals and sales targets. His company is very successful, but he wanted to take the sales side of the business to the next level.

Most of the opportunity for growth was around execution in the sales process. Deals were sometimes going sideways at the last minute because the scope was increasing and the decision-making process was not being validated with the customer early enough in the sales campaign. Andrew wanted to have his team focus on uncovering the decision-making process very early in the customer-engagement life-cycle. He wanted to have his team solve big problems for customers and take the time to be even more consultative. (This problem is by no means specific to this company or companies of any size—it is pretty much universal.) Andrew wanted his team to focus on a core set of questions about decision-making processes, compelling events, timelines, and any red flags that could derail projects.

We dove into the project together, starting by compiling a list of people in the organization to gather perspectives from. We lined up a couple of salespeople, a couple of sales-engagement managers, and the head of services. We also talked to a customer. We believed we had a good sense of what the solution needed to be, but it was invaluable to talk with these folks—especially a customer. Besides finding some great best practices and tools we could include in the project to become part of the company's sales values, we also used the interview exercise as a way to align the team. They all became part of the solution.

We followed a conversational interview style, starting with their view of how things were working today. They shared what they thought was working and what they thought could be improved. We learned so much from their stories and experiences. For example, one of the salespeople shared how she had just had a new decision maker show up last minute and push out the signing of the agreement; the issue was real and fresh. We had the salesperson share that real-life example during the launch of the new sales values.

With the interview information and a validated hypothesis, the core team met to brainstorm the creation of the sales values. We used a conference room and a big whiteboard, and we started by talking about what we heard and learned from the team. We put words on the whiteboard, and as we did, themes started emerging for us: words that would become anchors for the sales values. We listed out words and phrases like *business issues*, *discovery*, *decision-making process*, *mutual action plan*, *storytelling*, *credibility*, *customer communications*, *solving problems*, and *wowing the customer*. We looked at the words and found one that seemed to pull all the values together in an inspiring and directive way: *engage*. We began working the values around that word. (Note: Once you find a core word and have clarified the basics of the values you want your team to live by, a thesaurus becomes very useful in coming up with those memorable acronyms.) Here is where we ended up:

Explore their issues.

Navigate their company.

Grab their attention.

Ask for the money.

Grow their business.

Earn their trust.

Each of these sentences has a distinct meaning that encourages activity, expectations, and metrics. *Explore their issues* reminds the team to do a detailed discovery and to understand the client's critical business issues. *Navigate their company* helps the team to focus on all the influencers and stakeholders, making sure they all have a voice. *Grab their attention* brings focus to the professionalism of communications, including action-item lists, summary emails, presentations that wow, and proposals that are professional. *Ask for the money* reminds the team to stay focused on the decision-making process and evaluation criteria. *Grow their business* is about quantifying the value of the services to drive a return on investment. Finally, *Earn their trust* is about sharing customer stories, references, and examples to drive up confidence.

Next, we mapped the values to the sales process and ultimately brought it to life with sales tools, technology, manager reports, and training. We quickly applied the "engage" values to every deal conversation and customer interaction. I sat through their weekly deal reviews as an observer to help make sure "engage" came to life. I heard the salespeople themselves asking for more training and tools because they believed in this new way to sell. The "engage" values formed the foundation for all conversations, training, and weekly deal-review meetings.

• • •

Taking the reins of your role as an entrepreneurial sales manager starts with a strong set of sales values, and I hope you're excited to start the process with your own team. I hope you are realizing the importance of creating your own sales values regardless of the size of your team. Once you have those values settled upon, you're ready to start winning as a team—the subject of the next chapter.

CHAPTER 3

WIN AS A TEAM

With your sales values in place, you've laid the foundation for collaboration, mutual support, and a shared vision among your team. If you want truly stellar results, then transform your team from independent sales operators into a cohesive team and part of a sales community. Remember: A sense of community—and the connectedness and mutual learning that goes with it—is what leads to fully developed salespeople (that is, SalesHood). This means that goal sharing, transparency, communication, and alignment around common values can change everything for a sales team and take a group of employees from partially meeting their quotas to operating like a well-oiled sales machine with everyone blowing out the quota month after month.

It starts with the group of sales reps working directly under you, but the team we're talking about in this chapter and throughout the rest of this book can easily grow to encompass your sales support staff, your headquarters supporting staff, your external network, your partners, and even your customers. At this point it becomes more like a community. Remember, as an entrepreneur, you need to think about all aspects of the business, and that means fostering teamwork not just among your direct reports but also among them and everyone they interact with inside and outside the company. As three directors from the Corporate Executive Board Company (CEB) write in *Harvard Business Review*, "Exemplary sales managers serve as connectors within and beyond their teams, encouraging collaborative strategy development and problem solving."[9] The bottom line is that you have to *connect the dots* for your salespeople and this larger community to help them succeed. "It takes a village," as they say, and your experience and network will define who is in your sales team's village. Sales managers have frequently shared with me the importance of helping salespeople become knowledgeable about whom to go to for what when executing their deals. Many times at salesforce.com we would bring the entire sales team, including all extended members, on stage at sales kickoff events. I remember at one sales kickoff, when we wanted to highlight the importance of the *village* concept, we had over 140 people thanked and brought on stage. It took awhile to get everyone on stage, but the message was clear.

In business, communities—again, spanning employees, partners, and customers—are brought together based on common goals aligned by department, division, interests, identity, and projects. Henry Mintzberg wrote that communities require "leadership that intervenes when appropriate."[10] For the sales manager, this isn't an easily accomplished task, but if you fortify your entrepreneurial spirit and take responsibility for turning your team into a true community, you'll reap rich rewards.

A great entrepreneurial sales manager fosters a culture of "winning as a team"—something many people talk about but few put into practice. "Win as a team and never lose alone" is a great mantra to instill in people; it is the cornerstone of a team's success. Remember, it's up to you, the sales manager, to set the tone for the team. You want your group of reps to make up a thriving ecosystem. You want them to be colleagues and mentors, all inspired and motivated to help the team succeed. A few sales managers I've known have turned this into a science, and many of them are the inspiration for this book.

The concept of working together as a team and as a community really comes to life under a sales manager's leadership. The sales manager, the CEO of his territory, knows that he owns the success of his team and that that success depends upon the strength of the relationships within the team and community. For the team to be successful, its members must be able to count on each other and to rally resources to deliver on customer needs. When I ask successful sales managers what foundational success criteria exist for new sales hires they all mention the salesperson's ability to know who is who at headquarters. In other words, they want people to be able to create and navigate relationships with their team and resources around the company. They want people who keep an open line of communication between themselves and the valuable headquarters resources and with their team members.

INVEST THE TIME TO KNOW YOUR SALES TEAM'S SKILLS

Based on what I've seen over the years and what I've heard from talking to many sales managers, the vision of a super salesperson is usually a combination of many salespeople. They say, "It would be great if we could combine a few of my salespeople into one." When you build a cooperative team, that's precisely what you're doing— you're combining the best attributes of your best people to reach maximum effectiveness.

There is power and impact in taking the time to understand the individual strengths and weaknesses of your salespeople. Great sales managers provide constructive feedback and proactive career guidance, and they nurture mentorship across teams. That starts with taking the time to pause and do an honest and constructive assessment of a sales team. Trust me, it will have far-reaching benefits.

When I ask sales managers how they are doing their personal and team assessments today, many will say, "I do it, but it's ad hoc." They'll also say, "I have a clear picture in my head of the strengths and weaknesses of each salesperson on my team." One even told me that he keeps a journal of names with details on each person.

If you don't take the time to document your team's strong and weak points, you'll find it nearly impossible to begin gelling them into a cohesive team. I remember working with a sales manager to begin planning out her team's sales productivity program. We started by first talking about her goals and priorities. She shared that deals were getting stuck. The quantity of "no-decision" deals was high. Deals in the pipeline were "nice to have" but not mission critical. Sound familiar? We could have gone down the path to talk about the quality of leads or the corporate messaging, but the answer was not there. We had to start by helping this sales manager be honest about her team's skills and where the opportunities for improvement existed. She knew what we needed to do but hadn't taken the time to properly reflect on what was happening in her business.

We looked at the entire team, evaluating every salesperson. We recognized that her team was a new one with a lot of great energy and basic sales skills. They had good domain, and the product training was working. But what she realized was that her team lacked the ability to have in-depth, strategic conversations with prospects about critical business issues. They lacked the confidence and the competence. They were not creating qualified opportunities. After completing a team assessment, she realized that she needed her sales team to go deeper in their qualification and discovery conversations.

We created a sales program for this team focused on some core selling skills, including qualification conversations, open-ended questions, and discovery skills. The team embraced the focus and attention. We launched the program in a series of weekly team meetings we called "sales huddles" across a four-week period. We didn't fly the team around and use up precious selling time out of the field. What happened was that this sales manager solved the problem at the sales rep level by looking at how each salesperson was doing and then creating a program personalized to her team, which quickly began performing better. Their confidence improved. They were able to prioritize their time and focus on more qualified opportunities. Each person started having better conversations. They were asking richer questions and getting great answers from their customers. If someone was talking to the wrong people, then the team was quick to mentor better practices during their weekly team meetings. The sales manager used the information from the assessment to deliver personalized coaching to the team.

Because this sales manager took a focused approach to understanding her team's strengths and weaknesses and then provided a tailored program that helped them all come together, her team was appreciative and saw the thoughtful program as one that would help them achieve their full sales potential. She now knew what her team was capable of, and they were clear on where they needed to grow. The team was now growing together and, increasingly, winning together.

Take the time to assess each person on your team and look at his or her relative scores. Identify mentors and connect them with folks who have areas where growth is needed. Identify "hot spots" that need attention and build a plan to improve your salespeople's skills and performance. Be consistent, conduct this team assessment monthly or quarterly, and keep your suggestions and feedback actionable.

Here are some places to start with an assessment of your team. When you're familiar with how your people rank in these core skills, you can start bolstering their collective weak spots and encouraging the type of peer-to-peer mentoring we'll talk about in the next chapter.

First, how is your team doing on prospecting? Dive into a review of prospecting strategy, activity, communications, and use of social channels. Are your salespeople sending out impersonal email templates, or are they tailoring their prospecting outreach strategy to buyer priorities? Are they conducting the right quality and quantity of email, voicemail, and call-connect activities? (We'll get to more specifics on prospecting in chapter 10.)

Next, how are they doing with discovering key information about their prospects? Do they ask open-ended questions? How effective are they at going deep on an issue and quantifying its impact on the business? Do they ask probing, layered questions? Do they validate what they heard in their customer meetings in person and in email? (More on this in chapter 11.)

Are your salespeople using storytelling to highlight key selling features? (We'll explore that topic in chapter 12.) Do they handle objections and plant competitive traps effectively (chapter 13)?

The list goes on: Are they good presenters? How is their elevator pitch? How about their knowledge of the product they're selling? How do they handle boardroom style customer presentations? How are their closing skills when it comes to negotiations, deal structuring, and proposals? Are they writing compelling proposals that wow their customers?

These are just a few of the many potential areas where you can assess your team. The intent here is to push yourself to think even more holistically about your salespeople across a broader set of skills.

When you start managing them like an interdependent, comple-
mentary team, they'll follow your lead and start acting more like one.

IT TAKES A VILLAGE

As touched on earlier, a successful sales manager will turn her team
into a real community that extends beyond her direct reports and
includes the active participation of key contributors from other
departments in the company, including finance, legal, marketing,
and services.

I witnessed the magic of building a community of sales team
supporters. I was often invited to join the regional team meetings
led by the different sales managers. I was able to see how team
meetings were executed across a wide range of sales managers.

Dan Dal Degan (DDD), an accomplished sales executive I
worked very closely with at salesforce.com, ran great team meetings,
which he called "sales huddles," a great cultural stamp that really
exemplifies team building and the notion of a community. What was
unique to me about the way DDD ran his meetings was how he created an agenda and assembled folks from across the company. He
understood the importance of making those connections between
his sales team and the supporting team members who were indirectly motivated to help the team. Product leaders would attend
to educate his team on ways to sell new products. Field marketers
would attend, as they were motivated to drive up lead generation in
partnering with the sales team to launch marketing events. Partners
would attend to help propel customer success together. Finance and
legal would attend, too, as they were motivated to make sure that
proposals, contracts, and orders were processed correctly. There was
always a social component as well, where teams would be able to
network with one another.

DDD used his sales huddles as a way to make all the resources

known and available to his team in a very empowering way. It
increased their confidence. His team always felt blanketed by
resources from the company focused on making them money. I
look to DDD's sales huddles as a best practice and one that should
be part of the entrepreneurial spirit of every team.

There are many dimensions to this story that are relevant to
the entrepreneurial sales manager. First, it takes vision for a sales
manager to have a master plan of all the resources and people
required to make a team successful. DDD understood where he
and his team needed to put some emphasis to grow the business.
More importantly, he brought together experts who could help
his team fill those gaps. Secondly, it takes strong relationships and
relationship-building skills to be able to pull together a diverse
team of people who are indirectly aligned in an organizational
matrix. Consider the amount of work required to rally the folks;
you have to reach out to them, entice them to join the team
meeting, and then muster the charisma necessary to keep such a
diverse group motivated and inspired to contribute to the greater
good of the team's success. DDD did all of this with great skill.
He's an inspiration to every sales manager who wants to help her
salespeople win as a team!

TEAM SELLING

In many industries and customer engagements, salespeople have
a team-selling model where they pull in resource people such as
product managers, partners, and executives to help close deals.
Winning as a team is a common value across many high-technology
companies, especially in the enterprise-software world. An important part of team selling is pulling together the right resources and
tools during deal crunch time. Top performing salespeople all have
the ability to build a network of resources inside and outside their

company to help them achieve their goals. Resources can include anyone in the organization directly involved in helping to close deals; mentors who coach, advise, and provide insight; and even external parties such as partners. Introduce your salespeople to the idea of building their networks from the first day of their careers. Good salespeople usually have their extended network members on speed dial.

It's the job of the sales manager to coach and mentor the team, and to help them know when to pull in resources. Make it easy for them to do it; provide examples of successful salespeople and winning deals and showcase the teams it took to win. Celebrate the wins and the teams who made it happen. "Never lose alone."

It's also the job of the sales manager to build a culture of best practice sharing across the team. The best salespeople are those who know how to find and use the resources around them to deliver the highest value to their customers and prospects.

The sales team should share their best proposals and presentations with each other. In weekly meetings and sales huddles, it's the job of the sales manager to highlight top sales tools and successes with the broader team. This requires being on top of all the deal details and then knowing when something needs to be shared broadly.

For example, I was excited to see sales teams build their own list of customer stories and sales references outside of what their marketing organization provided. It takes an entrepreneurial sales manager to realize that a library of sales references is one of the most critical assets that a salesperson needs. Consider how important references are inside a sales process: Customers today want to speak with other customers like them. It's the job of the salesperson to ensure that they have enough of these references for team members to provide to customers, and it's the job of the sales manager to make sure that the sales references are being nurtured and not being overused by the sales teams.

Rallying resources is not easy to do. First you have to know *what* they are, and second, you have to know *who* they are. Both questions need to be answered in the context of a sales process. One of the things we did at salesforce.com to help sales teams gain access to tools and resources was to build teams of shared services. The sales teams appreciated the support. Shared services were created for requests for proposals (RFPs), business cases, demonstrations, executive briefing centers, and sales references.

The RFP team would work with the sales teams to create professional RFP submissions to customers. Every proposal would be amazing—each armed with a library of questions and answers and each written and designed by creative professionals. The demonstration team would create technically complex and graphically impressive customer-facing demonstrations, thus letting the sales teams focus on the actual selling. The business-cases team would build compelling value for customers. They had the spreadsheets, customer benchmarks, and financial models to create sophisticated comparisons for customers. Finally, the sales references team would source new customer stories and make sure they were ready to take reference calls. The sales teams knew these services were available and they were able to request the support on a deal-by-deal basis. We dubbed this the "bat phone" for sales teams. The return on investment of these shared services was huge. These services were possible because the ROI to sales leadership was clear and the alignment of go-to-market and sales productivity was strong.

Such deal support services are great for sales operations and marketing to provide focused support to sales teams. Share with them the idea and have them bring it to life in your company—and don't forget to track the resultant ROI!

The deal support tool also became popular with other teams around the company. It gave teams in finance, legal, contracts, pricing, and marketing a way to be part of the extended team through the mechanism to request support when the salesperson needed it. Many companies implement similar services after they realize the funding, resourcing, and scaling benefits.

CROWDSOURCE DEAL STRATEGIES AS A TEAM

I enjoy being an active participant (or even a fly on the wall) in sales teams' deal reviews and quarterly business reviews (QBRs). With the right mind-set and the right framing of a discussion by a sales manager, magic happens. As sales leaders, I encourage you to consider applying "crowdsourcing" principles to sales team meetings and deal strategy discussions. Give everyone a voice. Crowdsource winning deal strategies by motivating everyone to participate. Be specific about how each salesperson constructively shares deal-based coaching feedback with his or her peers. Keep it light and make it fun.

Bringing the entire sales team together to talk deals has so many material benefits to your business. This is a great way to manage the forward pipeline and inspire sales teams to build their businesses together. The sales team's forecast becomes more accurate and more real. The quality of the team's pipeline improves where quality is measured by improvements in the gap between expected pipeline and closed business. Salespeople mentor each other on ways to execute a winning strategy in their deals. Salespeople share where they are in their deals and they learn from each other. Fellow team members ask the hard questions. Blind spots are exposed. Close plans are created or polished. Deals close faster.

Imagine this scenario. It's the beginning of a quarter. A sales manager invites the sales team to talk about their pipeline and deals in a regular weekly sales meeting. Normally, the sales manager would run through the deal list and have the sales team review what's in their sales automation system. Consider this alternative. Before jumping into the deals, the sales manager selects a topic or theme to discuss that is relevant to the go-to market or what's going on with customers at that time.

For example, in Q4, good topics to consider reinforcing include compelling events, close plans, or decision-making processes. Best practices on the topic are first discussed, and then the deal discussion happens.

A new context is set for the team's deal review call. Each salesperson shares his or her deal strategy for active deals. A short deal story highlighting the most critical information is shared by each salesperson. Each salesperson presents for two minutes, then gives each other feedback and coaching comments.

These kinds of peer-to-peer deal conversations help salespeople realize what they know and what they don't know about their opportunities. Realistic expectations can be reset about winning, and action plans can be quickly created. Salespeople appreciate this "safe" forum to learn from each other and improve deal strategies. It's amazing to see how salespeople are willing to give each other sound advice about winning deal strategies. Who said that sales teams aren't motivated to help each other?

Here are some coaching comments that salespeople shared with their team in a real-life deal review that I joined. They represent crowdsourced deal advice in action.

- "Politics are too big to overcome. Push the deal."
- "Do you have a business buyer that will trump IT?"
- "My concern is access to power and confirming budget."
- "Are they going to spend the money?"
- "Use case would need to be more compelling."

- "What's their alternative? Suggest you highlight how spending time and money with disparate agencies and internal marketing teams will have less impactful results."

You can't buy this kind of peer-to-peer deal coaching on deals. Each of these comments is like gold, highlighting focused new actions to be executed immediately on deals.

BUILD EXTERNAL NETWORKS

A third area of community extends beyond the immediate team and the corporate boundaries and out to an external network. Sales managers who reinforce the need for all of their salespeople to build their outside networks using LinkedIn, InsideView, and similar social-networking tools know how valuable it is to have their team members connect with employees, executives, and partners outside the sales organization.

Do not underestimate the power of LinkedIn as a tool to help salespeople build their network. I am a believer and an active user; LinkedIn is a very important tool for me staying connected with companies and people I have worked with over the years. Many see LinkedIn as a recruiting and prospecting tool, but it is truly much more. Every time I have a conversation with a sales team about team selling, I always ask the same question and the answer is surprisingly consistent. My question is, "How many of you in this room are connected on LinkedIn with your direct team members?"

My follow-up question is, "How many of you are connected on LinkedIn with your executive staff?" Why? Because your external network is only as effective as your ability to connect it appropriately with your internal network.

It always amazes me how few connections exist within a sales team and then across an organization and its external partner network. Here are some tips you can take back to your teams. First, make sure that everyone on the team is connected. You should connect with your entire management chain and your executive team. You should also connect with your board members and your company advisers. You should connect with folks in marketing and products. Basically, connect with everyone in your extended network.

Allocate time in your next team meeting to have people on the team spend time making sure they are connected. You can easily create and distribute a list of names of people to connect with on LinkedIn. It is also a good idea to let the executives know your team is doing this so they can promptly accept their connections.

• • •

Sales team collaboration is a critical part of every sales organization's success. It starts by assessing the strengths and weaknesses of the current team, including the direct-selling staff and the indirect sales teams. Winning as a team implies embracing the power of internal and external networks. Tools like Linkedin are amazing multipliers that help your teams expand their networks by connecting with each other. Adopt the mantra: Never lose alone, and always win as a team.

CHAPTER 4

NURTURE SOCIAL LEARNING

Developing the skills of sales teams is a top priority, even for CEOs. It's great to see new titles like "chief learning officer" become sought-after positions with material impact on revenue. Applying the right kind of sales skills development and education programs should be a differentiator and a must-have for every sales team. But the term we usually use for this type of education—*sales training*—conjures up images of expensive third-party consulting engagements, long days (and sometimes weeks) spent listening to tediously delivered PowerPoint presentations, and sales training content that is mostly forgotten by the time participants get back home. Today, there is a revolution happening in the sales world. Given the advent of social and mobile technologies, salespeople are expecting more from their learning experiences. They are asking for training that is relevant and immediately usable without having to spend days and weeks away from field selling.

And yet the fact remains that every salesperson wants and needs to be trained, or to refresh skills, even the seasoned ones. The skill

level of your reps directly affects their ability to close deals, and as
sales manager you're positioned to fill the gaps in their sales education. According to an article written by members of the marketing
department ata DePaul University in the *Harvard Business Review*,
"Thirty-nine percent of B2B buyers select a vendor according to
the skills of the salesperson rather than price, quality or service
features."[11] The article goes on to share that "among sales personnel hired over a 10-year period, those coming from sales education programs hit the break-even point in their territories thirty
percent faster."

Companies today are struggling to offer their sales teams skills
and product training that is relevant, compelling, and impactful—
and that keeps them engaged. How can you strike this balance with
your own team? As sales manager, it's up to you to drive a culture
of continual learning; every moment needs to become a learning
moment. You should look for ways to harness the energy and experience of your team to propel real-time learning and to encourage
your people to spread and share best practices. No one else is going
to keep your team up-to-date and equip them with what to sell and
how to sell. You can't just hope that people will learn by osmosis.
If you want to distinguish yourself in the organization, step up and
deliver your own learning programs that are collaborative, action
oriented, and revenue generating. The new way should result in an
ongoing education program that your sales teams appreciate.

THE OLD WAY OF SALES TRAINING

Don't worry: This chapter won't be a cut-and-dried lecture on hiring trainers or leading seminars. Instead, I want to show you the
exhilarating new possibilities at your fingertips. Old-style training
and learning is on its way out, and a new vista lies before us.

I've sat through a ton of training programs over the course

of my career, and an alarming number of them missed the mark completely. I've seen teams cooped up in rooms for pricey daylong, even weeklong, sessions that delivered marginal (or no) results. I'm sure you have, too.

These sessions usually failed because they displayed the hallmark traits of old-style training. First, they delivered information via a one-way path: from instructor to student. The instructor is assumed to know things that will benefit the salespeople in the classroom. As we'll see in this chapter, this is far from the best environment for learning. Second, they jam as much information into the agenda as possible, under the assumption that the more topics they cover in the workshop, the better off the salespeople students will be. But there's only so much a person can absorb in an hour or even a day. When you're in an information-overload session, it's like trying to drink from a fire hose. The trainees lose focus; their eyes wander to the window or their smartphones; they start thinking about how many sales they could've made were it not for this blasted mandatory training session. . . .

Thankfully, there's a better way.

THE NEW WAY: SALES TRAINING IN THE TWENTY-FIRST CENTURY

It's my firm conviction that salespeople learn best when they're *learning from each other*, not when they're stuck in the traditional teacher-student scenario. The trends of video, community, mobile resources, and peer-to-peer mentoring have taken over. Now it's time to embrace them and apply them to your team. When you scratch the old way of training in favor of a more evolved approach, you'll see your culture flourish and your team's productivity skyrocket. And more importantly, everyone will have more fun.

In the following chapter, we'll build a road map for how you're going to train your team, but before we get there, it's important to build a foundation of understanding about how core assumptions about sales training have changed. Let's look at some of the big new concepts of twenty-first-century sales training.

Just-in-Time Learning

The power of technology is driving a huge shift in the way salespeople expect to learn. Content that would have normally been delivered in a workshop setting by product managers, marketers, and other experts can now be delivered through videos in an online environment, which makes it easier for reps to access content "just in time"—or at the precise moment when it will be most effective. Kevin Spacey said, in the context of the revolution happening in the world's broadcast networks, that we should "give people what they want, when they want it, in the form they want it in."[12] These principles apply to the world of sales education, too. More and more sales managers and sales trainers are asking themselves, "Does this content need to be delivered in person? Or can it easily be recorded and delivered to salespeople when they need it or when their sales manager wants them to watch it?"

The power of video is not only shifting content from classrooms to an online experience, but it is also introducing new ways to "chunk up" the learning. For example, rather than thinking about a three-day workshop, it makes more sense to think about three modules delivered across a number of weeks in a set number of hours per week. This dramatically reduces the amount of time out of the field for the salespeople. It also gives them a chance to apply the skills in real time on their active deals. Finally, it provides a forced mechanism to consume smaller amounts of information and new skills across a longer period of time. Retention is dramatically better, and qualitatively, sales teams are just happier. They don't feel like a jam-packed agenda is being forced on them. The typical complaint from sales teams after a multiday or weeklong training program: "Way too much covered."

Mobility

It is almost funny to include mobility as a learning trend, since it is so obvious, but it would seem negligent of me not to cover it. Every salesperson has a mobile device that can easily present videos and allow him or her to engage in learning from anywhere. Mobility has created an environment where sales teams can easily have conferences together, anytime and anyplace. Salespeople are doing team meetings from their home offices or anywhere for that matter. The ability to share and consume small amounts of information from a mobile device has turned idle time into productive time. It is critical that when this time presents itself to your salespeople that they can easily start learning anywhere and anytime.

Salespeople Learn from Salespeople

We have seen a huge shift in training from book and classroom to social, group-based, and community-based learning. I was first introduced to the idea of community-accelerated learning by watching a TED talk by Chris Anderson.[13] The gist of this concept as applied to the sales world is that salespeople learn best from peers who have experienced similar scenarios. Your reps want to learn from people who have been in their shoes and can share some insight that is real and immediately usable. Of course, you—the sales manager—aren't absent from this scenario. It's your job to facilitate social learning across your team by fostering a culture of coaching, mentoring, and sharing of best practices.

Community-accelerated learning happens when salespeople learn from each other and improve their skills by seeing what others are doing, and a successful sales manager will help enshrine team sharing as a centerpiece of the sales team's culture. Imagine a salesperson who has an experience with a customer and shares an "aha!" moment with the group automatically as it happened. Imagine thousands of salespeople connected to one another like a set of networked computers. The idea of community-accelerated learning is that salespeople learn, then act, then share, then refine, then learn more. The loop, just like the learning, is never ending.

The concept became very real for me in 2010 after embracing social learning as a catalyst to accelerate a major sales transformation initiative. The challenge in front of the team was to train the global sales organization on an updated sales process. We built a case study simulating a real-life selling scenario. We devised a team-based, competitive exercise to empower learning and encourage a competitive, winning spirit. The competition started in San Francisco and made its way around the world, city by city.

Here is where the story gets interesting. I remember standing in front of the first workshop class we ran in San Francisco, *reminding* the workshop participants not to share the case studies and the winning presentations with their peers around the world. (I had not yet embraced social learning.) But within minutes, the teams from the first workshop in San Francisco started sharing their materials with salespeople in other cities. I remember feeling mortified: All the hard work we put into creating the workshop would be lost when the secrets were revealed. *There goes our training*, we thought. Still, there was no way to stop the sharing. It had gone viral, because the teams were proud of their work and they wanted to share their lessons and best practices with their fellow salespeople around the world.

The next day we ran another workshop in which the folks in the room had seen the postings from the previous workshop group. But the end result wasn't what we expected. The second class was *much more prepared* than the first class. This trend continued for weeks. By the seventh week, the average workshop scores were 20 to 25 percent higher and the teams were much more creative and innovative. The scores were trending up workshop after workshop. Community-accelerated learning had come to life. We'd been focusing on the wrong thing by trying to keep salespeople from sharing. I got the message loud and clear: Salespeople learn best from each other.

Learning by Doing

Aristotle wrote, "For the things we have to learn before we can do them, we learn by doing them." Another great quote, this one from Benjamin Franklin: "Tell me and I forget; teach me and I may remember; involve me and I learn." These principles apply beautifully to salespeople and sales training. The most effective parts of sales training are those where salespeople share real-life deal scenarios and where they can demonstrate and apply their skills.

There's no comparison between giving a salesperson a lecture on a selling concept and showing him firsthand how it works. This ties in well with social learning: It's abundantly more effective for a rep to get walked through a selling technique by one of her peers who's used it successfully than it is for the same rep to read a few imaginary case studies crafted by a training company. Even better, when you're closely involved in training your reps, you can encourage them to try out new skills and concepts in their daily work and then come back together to share how it worked for them in the real world. That's the essence of learning by doing, and when it's coupled with social learning, everyone benefits.

CHANGE YOUR ASSUMPTIONS

Sales managers who are at the forefront of their fields are implementing these new concepts in sales training with their teams, and doing so gives them and their reps a clear competitive edge. Let's look at some of the implications this new way to execute learning has for traditional sales programs.

Annual Training Events vs. Manager-Led Sales Huddles

In the spirit of avoiding a fire-hose approach to learning that ends up boring and frustrating reps, more sales managers are instituting a culture and curriculum of modular learning. Instead of those weeklong retreats, they're leading shorter and more targeted training sessions that we call "sales huddles." The sales managers who have implemented this kind of training with their teams have appreciated it, sharing comments like: "That the course was spread over several weeks improved the extent to which my sales team retained the material. We had very high attendance rates and participation levels."

The intent of sales huddles is to take a curriculum and spread it out across a number of weeks to maximize learning, absorption, and consumption. Salespeople are able to learn new concepts and refresh old skills and then apply them to real-life deals and scenarios with real customers. More importantly, they return to the team and share how the new skill was used and what the feedback was from the customer. They can share the impact and get feedback in real time. Getting sales huddles infused into your sales culture and rhythm of the business is how you will grow and develop your team; it should be a personal goal of yours as an entrepreneurial sales manager. The companies that have executed have seen immediate improvements in sales effectiveness, pipeline quality, and forecast accuracy.

I was skeptical when I was first introduced to this concept. *How are sales managers going to train their reps?* I wondered. *What skills as trainers do they have?* After I spoke with many sales managers across a wide range of companies, it became very apparent that they were already doing this kind of knowledge sharing informally. What the sales managers really wanted was a structured framework for these huddles—powered by the spirit of coaching and mentoring—that would keep the team focused on what to learn.

I was quickly won over to the idea, and I worked very closely with Barry Rhein, a close friend and one of the world's greatest sales trainers, to roll out manager-led sales huddles at salesforce.com. The results spoke for themselves. The incredible benefits of huddle-based, manager-delivered input were consistently positive. Here are a few:

- Sales managers become better coaches.
- Training is scalable.
- Training is personalized for a team and individual sales-people.
- Salespeople's skill gaps are identified by their managers.
- Teams come together and are unified.
- Sales managers became better at their jobs.

One sales manager told me, "Sales huddles give me an opportunity to see firsthand where the individuals on my team are in terms of strengths and weaknesses."

I was working with a San Francisco start-up that wanted to improve velocity in their salespeople's deals. We decided that a refresher on compelling events—significant events that move a sale forward—was the right approach to drive urgency in their sales campaigns. During my pre-sales huddle interviews, the sales managers thought that spending an entire hour on training was overkill, but we proceeded anyway. After all, it was only a forty-five- to sixty-minute huddle, not a full day or week workshop.

We brought the team together to have a conversation about compelling events in their deals. The session very quickly turned into the equivalent of group therapy. We started with a discussion of the term compelling event itself, and I introduced the well-accepted industry definition: "A compelling event is a time-sensitive response to an internal or external business pressure that drives action within a defined time period with consequences of inactions."[14]

The team debated a bit about this definition, and we quickly aligned. Within minutes of starting the session, the salespeople were selecting their active deals and sharing the compelling event for each deal. Some admitted that they didn't have a compelling event. I remember some members of the group pushing back, and the discussion becoming quite heated. Some members of the sales team were adamant, for example, that a compelling event could be a month-end or a promotional discount, even though I believe that a compelling event is uncovered by asking customers questions about their business issues and uncovering their pain.

Using the industry definition, which the team had agreed on as a good starting place, the team voted on whether each deal really had a compelling event. It was remarkable; the room recognized that most of their active deals still lacked a compelling event. The more remarkable part of this story is that the room came to the conclusions together. They learned as a team what a compelling event is and is not. They reached a collective agreement on what it meant for their business and their deals. The sales manager was able to rely on the definition as a way to avoid friction and to not be perceived as the "bad guy." The net effect of this experience was a collective "aha!" about how to be more mindful of uncovering compelling events. Deal action plans became more focused.

As we reflected on the experiences, the sales managers and the salespeople were in awe of how active learning and group coaching had helped uncover compelling events. The magic was when the teams came to the conclusions themselves and the sales managers became the leaders inspiring learning.

This company and many others have embraced sales huddles

and community-accelerated learning rather than the traditional training retreats and as a result have seen skills improve, deals close faster, and win rates increase.

Ad Hoc Learning vs. Structured Peer Coaching

Many organizations treat coaching and performance management as an event that happens once or twice a year, but the beauty of peer coaching is that it *recognizes that every moment in a salesperson's day can be a learning moment.* Every activity and every interaction between a salesperson and her managers, peers, teams, and customers presents a learning opportunity. Why wait until a salesperson misses his quota to start coaching? Why not offer him coaching from his very first day on the job? Why not look for coaching opportunities beyond the actual sale and hitting targets? Making coaching social is the perfect way to enhance performance management and transform many salespeople for the better.

Peer coaching also recognizes that *different salespeople have different experiences, tenure, and knowledge* and therefore need different types of coaching. A successful sales manager will match salespeople to salespeople. The right person and people should deliver feedback and coaching at the right time. For example, say a salesperson is struggling with a specific sales skill, like prospecting or negotiations. One approach is to have that salesperson watch a video or read a document. Sitting down in a one-on-one session is good, too. An optimal way to get an even better result is to connect the salesperson with another salesperson who has the experience and can share real deal experiences around prospecting or negotiations. Being matched with the right mentor will highlight to the salesperson what to do and what not to do. It'll also give the salesperson an opportunity to ask questions he might not ask his sales manager or perhaps won't ask the team in a weekly meeting to avoid feeling like his question is too obvious.

Peer coaching also *drives scale*. More training and coaching can happen when salespeople fill in the training-resourcing gaps. With growing sales teams and training-resourcing ratios remaining flat, peer coaching becomes the only way to achieve scale and increase reach. Technology today enables peer-to-peer coaching to happen in scale.

Next, peer coaching *empowers engagement and participation*. Sales teams will be more active in the learning process if they know their peers will be giving them feedback—even more so if that feedback is given in a public, social way. It is one thing to receive a scorecard or test results that are private or even to sit in a room with a trainer and receive feedback. It is a completely different experience to have a room of salespeople present to each other and then share feedback with one another. The competitive dynamic that emerges pushes salespeople to perform better.

Finally, peer coaching *improves the quality of feedback* a salesperson gets. With the right instruction, salespeople will share constructive feedback that is very thoughtful. I have learned a lot about what to look for and what is important by listening to salespeople provide feedback to one another. (Salespeople who demonstrate a superior ability to provide constructive feedback for their peers can also be potential candidates for sales management.)

Sales Certification vs. Team Challenges

Over the years, I have seen many forms of sales certifications in which salespeople are "certified" by headquarters personnel. These experiences would have a salesperson stand and deliver a presentation to an expert with a scorecard in hand. Feedback is shared with the salesperson and the salesperson's manager. While this is a necessary evil in the world of sales training, it was instituted before the widespread adoption of social and mobile technologies. For the most part, when a sales certification program is rolled out, it's right up there on the list with root canals in terms of popularity with reps. Salespeople roll their eyes and wonder why there isn't a better way. As I take a journey back in time to all the sales certifications I was involved with, I have to smile, thinking about the many ways we rolled out certification programs to sales.

I remember when we created a new corporate presentation comprising eighty slides and a product demonstration that required more than ten hours of technical setup. From my office in San Francisco, I could hear the moaning from salespeople all the way over in Europe.

We set a deadline, and the most unproductive part was that we then sent a crew of "*experts*" around the world to certify every customer-facing employee. Each person had his or her time in front of the certification crew. I remember sitting there in a conference room in a city in Europe, looking at the schedule ahead of us for the day. We had a new salesperson coming in to complete sales certification every sixty minutes. That translated to at least ten sales certifications each day. It was brutal.

Needless to say, the overall experience was not positive. The sales teams felt like they were auditioning for something that was really not at the core of helping them make money. The marketing and sales productivity teams tasked with conducting the sales certifications over and over again felt like they were doing mundane, repetitive work. They were all way overpaid for what they were doing. The sales certification program's integrity was questioned. Though the statistics shared showed amazing sales certification numbers in terms of compliance, the sentiment across the sales organization about the program's impact was not positive.

Over the years, as we rolled out new sales productivity sales-certification initiatives, we saw some improvements. The programs became lighter and less audition-like. We reduced the number of hours salespeople needed to prepare for their sales certification, and we introduced new concepts that empowered sales managers to drive the sales certifications. But each sales certification highlighted different issues. For example, when we rolled out the manager-led sales certification, we uncovered that some sales managers were giving certain team members free passes. In some cases, the manager also got creative and gave the entire team free passes by having each salesperson present just one slide.

I remember thinking, *What is the right balance of keeping salespeople on message?* A company will define a need to have every salesperson and sales manager be on message with the latest corporate positioning and customer stories. I also wondered, *How can we increase accountability, integrity, and scale in the sales certification program?* Thinking even more deeply about this, I wondered how a sales-certification experience could be fun and optimize the educational impact.

I took a step back and started talking to many companies, sales managers, and salespeople to discover whether there was a better way. Inspired by what I heard, I determined that there was most definitely a new way to certify. The new way is based on salespeople *challenging* each other.

This new way can apply to certifying anything that can be captured in a document, proposal, or a video role-play. With today's technology, anything can be certified. The trick is, who certifies? Why not apply principles of collaboration and crowdsourcing to sales certification in order to ramp up accountability and transparency? Why not have the members of a sales team score and certify each other? If marketing creates a new corporate presentation with a supporting scorecard, video, and speaker notes, can't they empower the sales managers and salespeople themselves to be the stewards of sales certification? Is it possible that reputation could become the new certification?

The answer is yes. I was involved with a crowdsourced peer-scoring initiative with several companies. What I witnessed was amazing. The salespeople not only had fun watching each other's presentations, they also learned a lot more. The sales teams called this kind of learning and best practice sharing a "team challenge."

Consider the learning equation. I, as a salesperson, watch a marketing presentation on the corporate first call—I learn a bit. I then watch my sales manager deliver it—I learn more. I prepare and do my own video—that forces me to learn even a bit more. My learning increases exponentially when I watch two or three peers deliver the presentation themselves. I read through the comments that salespeople gave each other and I feel like I am reading a "best of" summary. The overall time commitment doesn't increase, but the learning impact grows exponentially with peer-to-peer social-certification programs.

As I observed these new team challenge initiatives, I saw folks sharing things they liked and highlighting what they learned from the different salespeople they certified. We accomplished scale, accountability, and learning like never before. Once again, by activating the sales team as a community and by drawing team members into meaningful interaction with each other, the sales manager fosters an environment where each team member can grow and mature toward being a fully realized salesperson—reaching SalesHood.

There are a few elements that need to be part of a team challenge initiative. First, you need an agreed-upon scorecard that captures the essence of the learning goals. Second, the team members need to be comfortable recording themselves on video. Third, the sales manager must lead the way, recording him- or herself first, setting the example.

For example, a company's first call pitch scorecard would include criteria, where a rating of one through five is selected for important sales skills like personalization, cadence, storytelling, objection handling, elevator pitch, business value, business issues, next steps, and product differentiators. You can use and adapt these criteria as a way to ensure corporate messaging scale and consistency.

• • •

Learning priorities continue to change as the economy changes, as new products are launched, as companies are acquired, and as new industries are tackled. As you develop your training strategy and your learning goals in the next chapter, consider that skills need to be refreshed and product training needs to be retaken, year after year. It is up to you to define the cadence and pace that is acceptable to your organization.

In the same way, the training needs of your sales team are going to evolve and change, sometimes rapidly. But as you adapt to new realities and employ some of the concepts of twenty-first-century sales training, remember one thing above all: Salespeople learn from salespeople. Your job, as an entrepreneurial sales manager, is to inspire as much peer-to-peer learning as possible.

CHAPTER 5

MAKE TRAINING RELEVANT

Now that you've got an idea of some new trends in sales training, I hope you're excited about implementing them with your own team. To help you do that, let's discuss a series of steps any sales manager can use to start owning his team's learning initiatives. This process will help you develop a training program that's impactful and well received by your salespeople. If you put some effort into following these steps, you'll be well on your way to creating a team of fully developed sales professionals. When you're stepping up and taking responsibility for training your reps—and helping them train each other—you'll be demonstrating leadership. You'll become an example of superior sales management that your peers will surely emulate.

STEP 1: ASSESS YOUR TEAM'S TRAINING NEEDS

The development of a training strategy for your team starts with an assessment of its current skills and competence levels. There are a number of ways to make this assessment. You can start by surveying your sales teams and having them self-assess themselves. You should ask them how they think they are doing and what they think they need in order to do their job better. Take a couple of minutes to review the section "Invest the Time to Know Your Sales Team's Skills" in chapter 3, focusing on the individuals and talents that make up your sales team.

Of course, your own observations of your team are important. Based on what you see on a daily basis, what are your reps doing well? What could they get better at? You can take it further by cross-referencing your observations and the team's self-assessment with customer feedback. Ask a representative sample of your customers how they feel your salespeople performed, and ask for specifics on what they did right and what they could improve. Look at their sales presentations and proposals to get a sense of how they are selling value.

If at all possible, you will also want to benchmark your salespeople against one another and against industry standards. Profile your top performers and your bottom performers and draw up a comparison between the two. You will quickly see trends in the experience and skills that will give you clues to tailor your training program. You will learn about their tenure, their work history, and their activities. You will begin to see trends in career progression and job history.

You can also gauge the success of your teams by modeling the performers' actual behaviors and then benchmarking them against all of your salespeople. Looking at actual sales data like win rates, activity trends, pipeline creation history, size of network, and other attributes can be very prescriptive if assessed properly. You can also work with your sales operations partners to get the information you need to make the right prescriptive coaching recommendations to your team.

Regardless of the approach, you should invest the time to gauge the competence and confidence of your sales teams so you can prioritize learning goals.

STEP 2: ALIGN WITH MARKETING

The next step in building a scalable training program is to map out a strategy that is aligned with your corporate goals. Understand your training goals and how they correlate with corporate priorities. Learning goals are critical to align sales teams with corporate priorities to ensure that the training delivered is pegged to measurable results.

And as you seek to align your team's training goals with your specific corporate ethos, environment, and strategic objectives, don't forget that partnering with marketing is a great strategy. It is the marketing department's mission to understand corporate goals and messaging and to communicate these important standards both internally and externally. They are the keeper of the brand. They are usually in sync with CEO priorities.

Consider the power of turning your training program into another brand channel for the CEO and marketing. The harmony here is to align marketing priorities with sales priorities. If you can forge these types of bonds between your team and marketing, you will convert your sales teams into evangelists for the overarching corporate message while also ramping up success for your team. Have this be a top training goal and you will realize the greatest possible win-win situations for you and for your company. I'm a big fan of partnering with marketing and channeling their amazing work for sales teams to use with their customers.

STEP 3: PRIORITIZE LEARNING PILLARS

As you develop your training program, create a set of core learning pillars that highlight what is most important to your sales team's success and what is most valued by your customers. Be transparent about what is more important and relevant. Regardless of industry and product, there are some universal truths in training that should be adopted. Your task as you put together your training program is to understand your most important sales skills and learning goals and assign a relative weight to each one, based on what you found during the assessment step. Here are five pillars that have consistently emerged as critical ones for many companies I know.

Pillar 1: Culture

Understanding your culture is key to helping your new hires represent your company and understand how to execute. This includes giving the corporate pitch and understanding who is who at your company. Teach your teams how to build internal networks so they can accelerate their achievement and drive customer success. I always made sure that it was front and center in every sales new-hire program.

Pillar 2: Product

Understanding your products and solutions must be a critical part of your training strategy. Note, however, that it is important to balance product training with the other learning pillars to make sure that you are not just training on your products. Take into account the need to train your sales teams on product and the need to retrain and recertify them when products are updated. All competitive training, including objection handling and competitive plays, are included in the product sections, too.

Pillar 3: Sales Execution

Take the time to go deep on the sales process and understand winning plays. Your sales process is the playbook your sales teams need to hit the ground running. Spend the time to walk your sales teams through customer stories and examples of how other salespeople were able to close deals. Be specific and very prescriptive.

Pillar 4: Sales Skills

For the most part, many salespeople believe they have already been professionally trained in selling. But I believe sales teams can always benefit from refresher training on key skills like prospecting, discovery, objection handling, storytelling, negotiations, and closing. The key is to find the right training rhythm and delivery that makes learning fun, social, and even competitive. Prospecting training is interesting to highlight, because many veteran salespeople do benefit from a refresher, given the rise of social media and social selling; it is not obvious to all salespeople how to use social media to prospect.

As a sales manager, it is important for you to focus on all steps in the life-cycle of salespeople, not just revenue attainment. Look at what salespeople are doing to get ramped up or to build their business. Dive into all aspects of how they grow their clientele. There are several activities that sales managers can use to coach their teams. These include onboarding, territory and account planning, sales execution, close plans, team selling, and skill development. Every sales manager should schedule time with salespeople to discuss their sales skills and growth areas—beyond just looking at pipeline. This should be a part of the culture of every company and every sales team.

Pillar 5: "Do My Job" Training

It is important that your sales teams have a clear understanding of what they need to do every day in their jobs. Expectation setting explains to salespeople what they need to do to be successful. Consider "how to" topics like:

- submitting a forecast;
- engaging sales support teams;
- building an account plan;
- logging sales activities; and
- processing orders.

These "do my job" learning categories are examples of building a training program that is relevant and will yield accelerated ramping of your sales new hires and ongoing development of your sales teams. The relative weighting of each pillar varies by company and results from doing the right research. Know your audience and your customers' buying expectations. Segment your sales teams and map their skills to your sales process.

STEP 4: DEVELOP THE TRAINING STRATEGY

Every sales manager will have her own training strategy, and it should be based on the plan for the year, as discussed in chapter 1, and the ranking of the five learning pillars.

The first question to answer is how much time throughout the year will be devoted to all training. All salespeople wonder how much time they will be spending each year in learning and training. There is a perception that every day in training is one day less selling and that the opportunity cost is too high. Based on my experience and industry benchmarks, I believe that a good amount of training,[15] including sales huddles, sales events, and all other training initiatives, is between ten to fifteen days per year. The number of days will go up and down based on complexity of the sales process, product offering, and go-to market.

Once you have a rough idea of how much time you're going to spend on training in the next year, you can use this information as a guide to help you create a training calendar for the year. Your people will rely on this schedule; one of the most frequent requests sales managers get is for such a calendar to be published, showing training topics by month or even by week.

One of the most underutilized times of the week is the weekly sales meeting. Part of building a training strategy is to incorporate this ever-so-important time into an overall approach to ongoing learning.

In order to bring this concept to life, I've created a calendar that serves as a framework to think about your year (see next page). Notice that it's mapped to business priorities. January is all about business development, with sales huddles geared toward prospecting and building pipeline. February is about rep readiness with a pitch certification program just in time for marketing's release of the new corporate presentation. The next phase is to focus on discovery, qualification, and pipeline maturation. The discovery sales huddles get the team focused on asking the right questions and being curious about their customer's business problems. The learning shifts in April to driving urgency in deals with a focus on compelling events and customer storytelling. And we finish the cycle of learning with a refresher on negotiations and mutual close plans. Each month ends with a focus on closing activities.

January

Week 1	Annual and Monthly Goal Setting
Week 2	Social Prospecting Sales Huddle
Week 3	Prospecting Sales Huddle Strategies (email and voicemail)
Week 4	Close

February

Week 1	New Pitch Preparation & Team Challenge
Week 2	Peer-to-Peer Scoring
Week 3	Critical Business Issues Sales Huddle
Week 4	Close

March

Week 1	Open-ended Discovery Questions Sales Huddle
Week 2	Value-based Discovery Sales Huddle
Week 3	No Sales Huddle
Week 4	Close

April

Week 1	Compelling Events Sales Huddle
Week 2	Decision-making Process Sales Huddle
Week 3	No Sales Huddle
Week 4	Close

May

Week 1	Competitive Objection Handling Role-play
Week 2	Customer Storytelling Sales Huddle
Week 3	No Sales Huddle
Week 4	Close

June

Week 1	Negotiation Best Practices Sales Huddle
Week 2	Mutual Close Plans Sales Huddle
Week 3	No Sales Huddle
Week 4	Close

The cycle of learning and collaboration can easily be repeated for the second half of the year. Sales managers can swap out sales huddle topics and themes for other ones, too.

When your basic sales huddle calendar is complete, flesh it out by outlining other types of training and specify how much time they will take and when they will be carried out. Map out every hour of learning, including videos, workshops, exercises, tests, and certifications, tying each one back to one of the five pillars. Of course, training should be focused on the pillars you determined were most important to your team. Laying out a full training plan is a painful and time-consuming exercise, but when it's done, it is always well received by reps, sales leadership, sales operations, and the stakeholders in marketing.

STEP 5: SHARE SUCCESSES BROADLY

To get the biggest benefit of your learning initiatives—especially the explicitly social ones—do your best to recognize and reward salespeople when they hit learning milestones. It's social; it's fun; it's engaging. Everyone loves to be recognized for a job well done, but salespeople tend to be very accomplishment oriented, so making sure you recognize their achievements in front of their peers is especially important here. Turn every result of the training program into a learning opportunity for everyone. Be transparent with positive outcomes and with outcomes that could have been improved. Social learning needs to be supported by an environment where it is safe to experiment and take risks.

At salesforce.com, we experienced some unexpected outcomes when we celebrated the success of one workshop we put on. A successful team participating in a workshop was recognized for a compelling customer presentation. While the exercise was just a case study, it still had a lot of reality in it. It turned out that the profile of the case study company matched a real-life selling scenario on the other side of the world. A salesperson in Canada reviewed the presentation created by the team in Australia and realized she could use it for a meeting she had with a customer the next day. That was the ultimate praise and never would have been possible if we hadn't broadcast this team's achievement in the workshop to the rest of the sales community. What a great example of training being relevant and immediately usable!

To realize this same benefit for your team, take the following steps for every social-learning initiative:

1. Develop leaderboards to showcase top performers and winners.

2. Highlight successes as they happen. First-line managers can make this happen effortlessly, because they are tied to every key deal.

3. Make sure to notify winners, their managers, and the broader teams.

4. Nurture a culture of best practice sharing and reward it.

5. Make it easy to find success stories and presentations.

• • •

Building a training strategy that accelerates a salesperson's success is very important to the health of your business. The principles in this chapter are intended to be applied by sales managers or, in larger organizations, in partnership with sales operations, sales enablement, and marketing. Start by knowing your team and driving a training strategy that maps to the rhythm of your business. Remember, every moment is a learning moment, and you don't have to rely on an annual event like a sales kickoff to train your sales teams.

CHAPTER 6

INSPIRE WITH COMMUNICATIONS

I remember reading a long time ago that communication is the glue that holds relationships together, and I believe it: Communication is critical to the success of every relationship, including those within a high-functioning sales team. Effective communications keep salespeople engaged, energized, and educated. The heart of sales productivity is to get the right information at the right time to salespeople.

Over the years, I've been inspired by many disciplines that have helped me develop a set of best practices around creating communications that are inspirational, appreciated, and action-oriented. Journalists and newspapers showed me the art of grabbing the attention of a reader with an eye-catching or punchy headline. Leaders in the high-technology industry, such as Steve Jobs and Marc Benioff, set the bar high with passion and persuasion. After attending many Tony Robbins seminars and working with him on a number of sales kickoff events, I became a believer in the power of "yes" and of action-oriented messages. Hollywood and the many movie directors I admire taught me the power of storytelling. (On this last topic, Andrew Stanton delivered a great TED talk called "The Clues to a Great Story."[16])

This chapter wraps all of those best practices into a set of tools you as a sales manager can use every day with your sales teams. Consider all the ways you're communicating today. My goal is to empower you to make every email, every team meeting, every one-on-one, and every other team interaction feel like a professional keynote delivered personally from you to each person on your team.

Don't let the internal spam that plagues so many corporations bring down your sales team's productivity. As a sales manager, it's your job to keep the noise level down and help your sales teams prioritize what is most important. As the leader of the team, you are responsible for translating and prioritizing for salespeople which communication messages apply to their accounts, sales campaigns, and territories. And, just as important, you're responsible for the other side of communication—listening to what your team tells you and acting on that information.

BUILD A COMMUNICATIONS STRATEGY

Being strategic about communication is not just for marketers. Being strategic means that at the highest level, the sales manager has a vision of the year, quarter, month, and week that correlates with the rhythm of the business and its plan for the year. For example, the focus of the first set of weekly meetings at the beginning of the year should be on building new pipeline and creating a large funnel of new business. The theme and all communications, tools, and conversations should be focused on that top goal to keep the team aligned and focused. Communications should also resonate with themes that you or the company have established. If you have a theme for the year—which, again, I highly recommend—make sure that you're consistently reinforcing it as you communicate with your reps. You might even take it a step further and publish a theme for the month. That theme could then show up on email subject lines, in weekly kickoff calls, and on a team calendar.

What you communicate is just as important as how you communicate it. The tone and crispness of the messages really set great sales managers apart from good ones. Some of the most successful sales managers I have worked with have taken great strides to make their communications professional and consistent. (As Pablo Picasso once said, "Good artists copy; great artists steal.") In the communities of sales managers I have worked with, some of the best ones always had great team meeting agendas, business review templates, and weekly motivational notes to their sales teams. Others were smart enough to know they needed these communication tools for their teams and used their sales manager friends and network to borrow winning meeting topics and internal team emails.

It's a best practice to kick off each month with a team call. Rally the team with an action-oriented and motivational note that is sent out through your regular communication channels, be it email, team group, or company social network. Hype up your month and what you want the team to accomplish. Be clear on the goals and keep the energy focused and fun. It's your job to excite and inspire the team.

Close out every month, quarter, and year with thank-you notes to celebrate the successes of the team. Congratulate the team on their great results. Highlight the highs and the team wins. Recognize top performers. Include the direct and indirect team members in your notes. Sending out congratulatory notes to thank members of extended teams for their huge impact on your team's success will make them want to contribute more. Recognize all wins, including pipeline, revenue, and customer success. I remember always appreciating being included in sales managers' month- or quarter-end celebratory notes to their teams. Just make sure that you're consistent; send out these wrap-up notes at each and every month end, quarter end, and year end. I always appreciated getting thank-you notes back from salespeople after I would send out an email message. As an aside, handwritten notes are a novelty these days, so consider integrating them with your communication cadence.

Use your resources and network to achieve your goals by having subject-matter experts augment your communication strategies. Bring in special guest speakers to your monthly or quarterly kickoff calls and team meetings. Keep the speakers and topics fresh and relevant. Consider engaging executives, product managers, or partners to help drive momentum around key business goals or themes of the month. When I was running a product line at salesforce.com, I could very quickly identify the sales managers who were hungry and which ones wanted to build pipeline and push their sales teams to sell more products. I knew this because as the product GM I was responsible for selling as much of the Partner Relationship Management product as possible. I did my tours, visited the regions, and trained the sales teams. But the sales managers who wanted to go that extra step beyond the generic training to something special for their teams would invite me to their team meetings. I would participate and spend ten minutes going a level deeper on the content and sharing how the product would generate pipeline for a specific set of salespeople covering a specific industry. These sales managers who went that extra mile were on the top of the leaderboards, and their salespeople were the ones on stage, talking about how they sold my product. It all started with the sales manager reaching out, being entrepreneurial, owning the outcomes, and inviting outside subject-matter experts to their team meetings.

Weekly team meetings or sales huddles are always happening. Sales managers around the world do them every week—or at least most of them do. The effectiveness of these meetings depends on the sales leader's ability to define and communicate an agenda to the team and then to execute the meeting. It's important to always have an agenda set before the meeting starts and to make sure there is a balance among reviewing deals and pipeline, sharing best practices, and learning. The meeting itself is a way to highlight priorities, deliver key messages, and explain new products. The sales huddle is really the only time in the week that the sales manager brings the team together as a group. The time should be used wisely and planned appropriately.

EVERY WORD COUNTS

There is a formula to crafting the right messages that grab the attention of salespeople and drive the right actions. Use email effectively by sending the right messages at the right time. For example, it's great to send a note to your sales teams on Sunday night or first thing Monday morning with a quick reminder of what to do to get the week started off right; you can post questions and make suggestions about spending time prospecting, qualifying, and closing. I like S. Anthony Iannarino's blog post called "10 Questions to Start Your Week." There are some good nuggets you can borrow to drive the right behaviors with your teams. Here are some pertinent examples: "What live opportunities in your pipeline can you move forward this week? How much time are you going to spend prospecting for new opportunities this week? What time are you going to block on your calendar for opportunity creation?"[17] When I focus on how to communicate a message, I follow a simple journalistic approach that reporters use in the newspaper and other media channels. I make every communication read like an article on the front page of the *New York Times*. I know it sounds a bit much, but it's true. This applies to every email that you send out to your sales team. They take every email very seriously, so watch every word and be wary of every email you forward without an explanation. Your job is to keep your team focused and selling, not to give them more stuff to read that will clutter up their already pretty noisy intake of blogs, tweets, emails, and anything else they read.

I love catchy headlines. The subject line of an email will do so much toward helping your team know what you're communicating to them. Use action words and keep the subject line punchy. Trust me, it works. Some phrases that may catch the attention of your salespeople are "close bigger deals," "sell value," and "build pipeline fast." These might seem a bit like spam material to you, but consider your role: You are their sales manager, and your email automatically gets prioritized. Use very action-oriented words. Salespeople would stop me all the time and say things like, "You know, your emails grab our attention and get read because the subject line pulls us into your content." You want your team to have a similar reaction to your emails and notes.

Somewhere in the message, it helps to have an image that captures the essence of your story or represents the message well. It is very easy to include an image in messages these days; it takes a few seconds to add. Use images that make sense and point back to your communication strategy. If you are focused on certain products or a certain activity like prospecting, including an image of the product, a screenshot of a report, or a team picture can help you quickly project your message. But more often than not, teams do not take advantage of this compelling communication tool.

Crisp Writing with Bullets and Bold Fonts

Keep sentences short and punchy. Use bullets. Assume that everyone is reading the note from a mobile device. Further assume that you have no more than two to three minutes before a salesperson hits "delete" or moves on to the next note. I also use styles, a common feature in writing and notepad applications, as a way to highlight sentences with bold or colors.

Clear Call to Action

Make it very clear what you want your salespeople to do with the information you are sharing with them. Include statements like "Click here to watch the demonstration" or "Use these plays in your territory starting tomorrow." Be specific and very actionable. It removes the guesswork and helps salespeople prioritize.

Links to Assets and Tools

Include links to tools, playbooks, and videos in the note. It is very easy for a salesperson to click through to a YouTube link or an internal service and get the detail on your message through a video.

Make It Mobile Friendly

As I said earlier, the underlying assumption is that everyone is using a mobile device. Start there and you will already be miles ahead.

Keep the Note Short

Less is more; only share the most important key points. Remember the attention span of a salesperson. I like the rule of thumb of trying to keep notes fewer than one thousand characters. Twitter has it right!

Drive the Drumbeat

Be consistent, and repeat messages over and over. For every communication, think about what the "drumbeat" strategy is.

A SAMPLE MEMO TO ENERGIZE YOUR TEAM

It's the last month of the year. It's crunch time. Inspire your sales teams with your communications in your team meetings and in email. There is no time like the present to inspire your sales team to think big and make the month and the year count. You're already on your way to a great year.

Here is a memo you can send out to your sales teams to ignite the end of year magic. Personalize it to your style and sales culture.

To: Your Sales Team

Subject: Make December BIG

It's our time. Now more than ever we need to focus our activity to make December and this year really count. Let's prepare for the 20th being the end of the month. Here are some priorities for you to think about in every deal and for us to talk about in our team meetings and one-on-ones.

Bubble Up Red Flags
Avoid "happy ears" and make sure we are being mindful of any red flags on our deals. Consider any last moves our competitors may do to try and derail a buy decision that's in our favor. Watch for influencers in your accounts that may have objections we need to overcome. Be curious. Don't be afraid to ask hard questions even if the answers may not be in our favor.

Sharpen Your Close Clans
Whether you call it a success plan or a mutual action plan, every deal should have a "Close Plan." Make sure your champions and influencers are aligned on the Close Plan activities. Empower your buyers with the close plans to achieve success. Use language in the Close Plans that is customer specific. Have your customers sign off on the document if they haven't already.

Look For Upside Deals

Don't underestimate the power of upside deals. Look at your Q1 opportunities for any upside. Your customers have issues and initiatives that need to be solved now. The magic of Q4 is alive in their buying cycles too. Solve big problems and uncover compelling events to accelerate opportunities.

Use Your Resources

Never lose alone. Win as a team. Your executive, product, marketing, and support teams are here to help you demonstrate value with your customers. Don't be afraid to request help for any of your opportunities. You have an army behind you ready to act on any need.

Avoid Deals Going Sideways

The last thing you want is a deal going sideways at the end of the month because we missed a step in the buying process. Have all the logistical details mapped out and known. These are important steps that should be included in your Close Plans too. Make sure the PO process, vacation time, legal hurdles and board meetings are known. Stay on top of your customer's decision-making process.

The entire company is here to help you and your customers be successful.

Make it count. Finish strong.

Happy selling.

LISTENING TO THE TEAM

So far in this chapter, we've been talking about how you can send information and ideas to your team. But this chapter is on *communication*, and communication is a two-way street. In other words, just as important as talking to your reps is hearing what they have to say.

We all know that salespeople are full of opinions. They have great ideas. The best ones are creative problem solvers. I have learned so much from salespeople and have used their input over and over to develop new sales productivity program ideas. Every time I connect with a salesperson or a sales manager, I'm looking for ways I can help make them more productive. I listen for clues to making their jobs easier. I watch for subtle complaints or frustrations. I take note of what can help make them more money. Every idea is a great idea; the real challenge is making them all happen. Be an active listener and add to your job requirements and day-to-day activities to always be listening to your sales team. Soak up the brilliance of everyone around you and then decide how best to implement it. In short, listen, engage—and then act.

A great leader listens to the team uncover new ideas, best practices, and process improvements. Sometimes what you hear will be constructive feedback, too. As a leader, you want to hear it all, and you want to make sure your team knows that you have an open-door policy.

Crowdsource Sales Tools and Best Practices

Many organizations across a wide range of industries are embracing crowdsourcing as a way to differentiate and make their businesses better. With advances in technology and more openness to social collaboration, sharing knowledge across teams is accelerating business growth. Relationships are being redefined. Governments are rethinking how they serve their constituents. Businesses are opening new markets they never dreamed existed.

Though the term *crowdsourcing* typically refers to enlisting large swaths of the Internet community for help in a particular effort or project, I encourage you to think about using the same concept within your team. The same benefits so many companies and individuals see from crowdsourcing are now open to sales managers who enlist their teams for help with creating sales tools and best practices. Nurturing a culture of crowdsourcing and rep participation has shown me how to really meet salespeople's productivity needs and deliver amazing sales programs. My goal is to help you embrace a similar philosophy in the way you run your sales team. Solicit your team's help as you build sales training, share best practices, collect sales references, build competitive plays, uncover process improvements, and much more. This form of crowdsourcing is an important part of your leadership, team culture, and communication strategy. Considering salespeople ultimately want to share their experiences and learn from each other, crowdsourcing them for tools and winning sales plays makes total sense.

You know you have succeeded with crowdsourcing your sales teams when they are using the tools they developed and are boasting about it. Crowdsourcing helps you and your leaders feel the pulse of what is going on in your sales organization. It helps you deliver programs and tools that are exactly what sales teams need, when they need it. In a very tangible way, it focuses on the voice of your sales team as the critical part of the sales productivity equation.

Take your tools to the next level by crowdsourcing updates and changes to them by your sales teams. The results will be valued and immediately usable. Why guess when your sales teams will tell you what they need? I remember one specific tool that emerged as a best practice: an executive close presentation. We had a number of tools already available to sales teams, but the executive close presentation emerged as a hybrid between a first-call corporate-marketing presentation and a well-documented proposal. The creation of this asset would never have been identified or shared had we not asked. There are many amazing jewels sitting in your sales community that are ready to be crowdsourced and shared across all your sales teams. Once again, this demonstrates the indispensable nature of community in the principles of SalesHood.

Listening to your salespeople is the heart and soul of a winning sales program. It's the secret to delivering sales programs that are compelling and timely and that provide real value to your salespeople.

Crowdsourcing ideas and best practices enables you and your teams to solve real problems and meet the needs of your stakeholders. It also gets you one step closer to the customer. I have learned so much from simply listening to the salespeople around me, especially when they're telling me what works for them and what doesn't.

Done right, crowdsourcing your sales teams provides a scalable way to collect new ideas that your sales teams will love and thank you for, over and over. Listening to sales teams will make them productive and solve their problems. It's all about paying close attention to the needs of salespeople and having your finger on the pulse of what they are feeling and saying. Build it into the culture. The assumption that every idea is a good idea needs to be at the core of crowdsourcing. By introducing the importance of crowdsourcing sales tools and new ideas, you will also become your marketing department's best friend, because you'll be giving them access to what's really happening on the street.

Crowdsourcing in Action

I was working with a company, helping them to ramp up their pipeline and prospecting skills. We decided to run a few sales learning huddles on social prospecting and outreach strategies. Part of the workshop was to better understand buyer priorities and map them to prospecting tactics like email and voicemail. The sales team was younger in tenure, with an average of less than seven years of selling experience.

It is always great to reconnect a team with a refresher on buyer priorities. The conversation was very fruitful. We then shared a strategy and rhythm for prospecting. Part of the sales learning huddle was a review of winning prospecting email and voice templates.

An hour or so later, I got a call from the sales team I was working with. They shared that they had finished. I did not quite follow *what* they had finished exactly, but I was all ears. They told me they finished updating the email and voicemail templates with their buyer priorities as they saw them in their market. They had developed the tools as a team. I was impressed. Normally, the email templates are created by marketing and handed over to sales. The sales teams then use them and don't really customize them to match to their prospecting strategies and buyer priorities. Instead, most sales teams will take the templates and make minor modifications, and the prospecting success will vary. But this sales team had taken the initiative to act on the ideas I had shared with them in specific ways tailored to their needs.

And what was even more impressive was the impact this had on their pipeline generation *the next day*. They were more confident, and they owned the voicemail and email messages. Callbacks, hit rates, and pipeline creation numbers all improved.

This illustrates the power of crowdsourcing in action, and it took this young sales team to show me that they wanted to build the tools themselves. I realized that this same crowdsourced development exercise could be applied for every sales skill: competitive objection handling, discovery questions, customer stories, and more. Why not engage sales teams more actively in the creation of the tools they need and will use?

• • •

Communication is the glue that holds relationships together. Remember that communication is two-way, and it's just as important to listen closely as it is to communicate effectively. Have an open mind when new ideas are brought to the table. Motivate your sales teams to give feedback and share best practices with each other. And be consistent in making your team meetings and notes so good that your salespeople will look forward to them, not dread them. It's up to you to set the communication tone across the team. It all starts with a well-thought-out communication strategy.

CHAPTER 7

MOTIVATE ACTION

The sales managers I have most admired are those who get consistent results from their teams while creating a working environment that thrives on respect, trust, and fun. These leaders' teams are loyal—to the point that when one of these sales managers joins a company, they do so with a posse.

How do they do it? When I see a sales manager like this, I know he probably has the right motivational programs in place. I know he understands how to make his team members push themselves to exceed goals without giving up the fun. His team members are believers because they understand what's in it for them. In a word, they're motivated.

The goal of this chapter is to build a framework for using motivational drivers like reputation, gamification, incentives, peer competitions, and kickoff events to ultimately grow the business. As the CEO of your business, you know the opportunity costs of taking your teams out of the field for days and weeks. Let's help you maximize the investments you make to bring your teams together by sharing key motivational principles. Whether you're a first-time sales manager getting ready to launch your first in-person team meeting or sales kickoff, or a veteran getting ready to host a five-thousand-person event, you'll find value in this chapter.

MOTIVATE THROUGH COMPETITION AND GAMIFICATION

There's nothing to fear in harnessing the competitive spirit to reinforce the right behaviors and motivate your teams. Competition comes in many forms. There are the obvious, such as leaderboards that chart revenue and correlate to big checks for top performers. Everyone wants to be on the top of the leaderboards. But there are other types of team-based competitive activity that will inspire and motivate your reps. Consider the impact of using competitive principles to improve relative sales skills and accelerate performance. Since we know salespeople appreciate learning from each other, find ways to bring that together with a competition. Use motivational programs and team events to have your salespeople show off their stuff.

When you bring a team together, rather than have them sit through hours of PowerPoint slides, why not have them come prepared to deliver a presentation? For example, in the sales engineering and technical worlds, it's easy to have salespeople prepare product demonstrations. For salespeople, have them come prepared to share their latest boardroom customer presentation. Have your teams *challenge* each other to show off their skills and share best practices.

The fear of not performing well in front of peers is a great motivator. Use that fear and energy to employ gamification mechanics that motivate action. Gabe Zichermann, a friend and industry thought leader in the discipline of gamification, writes, "Gamification is the use of game thinking and game dynamics to engage audiences and solve problems."[18] Today, many companies are looking to use gamification to drive their employees' results, and it's especially relevant in sales departments; motivating salespeople using gamification is a natural, given their raw, competitive nature.

Game theory enables businesses to apply the same principles that inspire people (and children) to play games to improve their performance and productivity. I appreciate the framework outlined by Tadhg Kelly in a TechCrunch.com article: "Only three kinds of gamification are generally worth pursuing. . . . They are: validation, completion, and prizes."[19] Consider the application to sales productivity. A validation game might involve a system where reps can vote on each other's presentation materials; the winning rep would thus feel validated. A completion game might see reps working to check off all the boxes next to steps along the sales process or competing to see who can get the most calls under their belt in a given week. And a prize game—the simplest of all—would see you handing out cash, travel, or other awards to the reps who exhibit the behavior you hope to see other reps duplicate.

A few years ago at salesforce.com, in the commercial mid-market sales segment, under the leadership of Brian Millham, we ran a sales productivity program focused on building pipeline with a strong focus on competitiveness inside and across sales teams. It's a suggested best practice to have top sales leaders articulate to teams the importance of a sales program by sponsoring them personally. Brian made the goals clear: Create qualified new sales pipeline, also known as net new business. We set goals by country, segment, sales manager, and ultimately by salesperson. The completion activity was fairly binary, as we measured the number of outbound sales calls and emails conducted and new business created. The key for this program was setting goals and making the attainment of the goals a team sport. The validation was conducted through automation to measure number of activities logged and leads or opportunities created. We also dove into quantity and quality of pipeline generated.

What was unique about this sales program was that the sales managers decided that the primary incentive would simply be the public display on the leaderboards. The sales managers were empowered with leaderboards for their teams that they shared frequently. The surefire way to drive the competitive spirit and boost participation is to share and promote leaderboards. No one wanted to be on the bottom! I remember getting a note from one of the salespeople asking if I could remove them from the bottom of the new business-generated leaderboard. Clearly I could not, as the leaderboards were automatically generated from actual sales activity logged. I ended up sharing that interaction with the salesperson in a subsequent training event to highlight that each salesperson controlled his or her own destiny and could be on the top of the leaderboard by making the calls and doing the work. Brian and his sales leadership team integrated these team challenges and competitions with how they run their business because they had such a material impact on pipeline and revenues.

The power of reputation is a big driver in the sales world. I see this a lot at many companies and sales teams. The notion of reputation is an anchor tenet of every sales manager's motivational tools. Using a reputation lever to recognize top performers—across all behaviors, not just revenue performance—is a great way to give everyone on your sales team a chance to be a star. It's the ultimate motivator—next to closing deals, of course. Salespeople like to be recognized. You can use themes like "best rookie" or "top pipeline generator" to reinforce behaviors. Pick themes that correlate with your team's culture and that will make sense to your salespeople.

INCENTIVE TRAVEL WORKS

An event type that helps to energize, motivate, and improve productivity of salespeople is incentive travel. I worked at Maritz, one of the largest incentive-travel motivation companies, early in my career and witnessed the power of these programs; I'm a believer! I carried the value and importance of carrots and noncash incentives such as travel with me in my sales career. Everyone knows that incentive travel is fun, and destinations like Hawaii, the Caribbean, or the Mediterranean are expected parts of a sales incentive program. In your communications, weekly meetings, and local events, reinforce the incentive-travel programs that are created by headquarters. Highlight top performers and use these programs as a way to give that extra push needed every month.

At salesforce.com, one motivational program in particular continues to receive off-the-charts feedback from the sales teams and their spouses. Every year at the Hawaii Club incentive destination, top performers are offered the chance to take their significant other on a shopping spree at a Tiffany's store. CNN described it this way: "The biggest earners get to enjoy goodies like 'Breakfast at Tiffany's'—a $5,000 shopping spree offered during last year's sales incentive trip to Hawaii. Since Tiffany doesn't have a store in Kauai, salesforce.com hired local carpenters to recreate one, shipped in $1 million in merchandise from surrounding islands, and hired a violin player, chef, and even Miss Hawaii to add ambience."[20]

A car service is arranged. Strawberries and champagne are served. A credit card is handed over to the excited award winner and their significant other to go shopping. The teams are then brought back to show off their goods. Every salesperson in the room and their significant other is saying to themselves, *I want to go shopping next year*. Breakfast at Tiffany's is a big part of the sales culture at salesforce.com and a very sought-after award.

USING SALES KICKOFF EVENTS TO MOTIVATE

Holding effective events with your team throughout the year is another cornerstone of keeping reps motivated and inspired. Sales kickoff events are the most common type of event. They might precede a new year and include the presentation of new initiatives and new sales goals, or serve as a great midyear driver to reenergize and align sales teams on top priorities. Sales kickoff events are great at building culture and sharing best practices across sales territories. Also, another type of event that effectively aligns and motivates salespeople is quarterly business reviews. Regardless of the size and scope of your team, you will want to have your sales teams experience inspirational talks, operational excellence, and fun times, too. There is a balance and you can achieve all with the right planning.

Once the decision is made that you're going to invest in an in-person event, your next step is to be clear on what you're trying to accomplish. While education is a top goal, it is sometimes difficult and not always advisable to have direct learning be the top focus of an event like a sales kickoff.

Consider the reality of what is about to happen. You are bringing your teams together for a few days. While some education is important, you can use your event as a platform to launch an educational program that spans multiple months and quarters. It sets the tone for a year. I recently worked with a start-up that wanted to use two and a half days of a midyear kickoff meeting to dive into core selling skills. Rather than assume that the entire sales team would learn all they needed to be better salespeople, we decided to introduce (or refresh) some skills. We used the midyear event as a platform to share what was most important and what we would be focusing on in the coming months. This worked well, because it didn't overwhelm the teams with too much information and empowered the sales managers with a learning road map that augmented the event goals. We followed the midyear event with waves of sales huddles executed by sales managers with their teams, reinforcing the priorities and educational goals. Plan every event to be inspirational, fun, and educational for every participant.

Events Start with a Vision

Hosting an event just for the sake of hosting one clearly is not in anyone's best interest. Time is so precious, and we want to make sure that we are adding value to salespeople's lives and careers through a meaningful events strategy.

The first place to start when beginning to plan for an event like a kickoff or a training event is with a vision statement. The vision should be supported by goals that are aligned with your executives' top priorities. Build a vision statement, much like a company has a vision statement. Then, share it broadly across your teams. The purpose of a vision statement is to align key executives, participants, and stakeholders who will help make the event successful. We create vision statements for every event we lead or participate in; these become anchors for marketing and product groups, as they are always major contributors of content.

Here are some sales-specific event goals that you can use to get started to inspire your own event vision statement:

1. Recognize top performers.
2. Inspire team selling.
3. Share best practices across sales teams.
4. Build relationships through networking.
5. Launch a new product.

You can use these goal examples to create action-oriented methods with specific tactics and metrics. Your stakeholders in building an inspirational sales event will appreciate the clarity, focus, and discipline. You will also have a much more impactful event, one where every speaker and every person developing content will be aligned with your program goals and vision. Every sales event and sales program should have a clear vision statement, complete with methods and metrics. Be clear on what it is you want to accomplish and measure it.[21]

For one of the sales events we ran, we identified relationship building, team selling, and networking as important event goals. We shifted our agenda and workshop themes from being "death by PowerPoint" to a lot of hands-on networking activity. We creatively used *"speed-dating-like"* exercises wrapped around the sharing of best practices in selling. For example, we developed a great in-person networking event mixed in with a bit of competitive spirit and education around customer storytelling. Let me share some tips that made this exercise a success.

The goal of the exercise was threefold. First, we wanted salespeople to meet other salespeople, to expand their network of mentors and resources. Second, we wanted salespeople to share their great customer stories, to arm their peers with more stories in their sales arsenal. Third, we wanted to enrich the database of customer stories in a scalable way. All three goals were accomplished.

We asked every salesperson to come prepared to share his or her top three stories. They were asked to write the customer stories down. When the customer-stories networking exercise happened, each person in each group had two minutes to share his or her customer story. The team voted for the best customer stories. By the end, every person had heard three new customer stories. The exercise itself provided the perfect icebreaker: Participants were able to show off their customer storytelling prowess. And finally, the richness of the customer stories database was improved. Such an exercise works well in person and also can work in a virtual setting. All in all, the motivation was high for the salespeople to get their stories organized and told to each other in a compelling way. The stakes were high, and everyone took to the challenge very seriously.

Apply Marketing Principles to Your Events

When you are tasked with creating a team event, you want to do more than just slap together an agenda. Take your vision, which should be based on business goals, and create a theme for your event. Themes are a great way to turn a regular, boring meeting into something magical. Hopefully you've set a theme for your year (as discussed in chapter 1); if so, you can have the theme of the event mirror or supplement the year's theme.

The power of a killer theme will set the tone for your entire event and all subsequent activities. It will become part of your team's culture and DNA. Be strategic and avoid being tactical. Think big. Use this opportunity to raise your game. Have fun. Remember that every minute your team isn't selling comes with a high opportunity cost, so make the most of it. Your team is looking to you for tone and intent. Keep it positive but actionable. Think about how you can change the psyche of your sales team. Take a chapter from our marketing leaders and note that the right theme can do that.

Over the years at salesforce.com, we chose themes that anchored our sales events in the goals of the company, and many salespeople told me how much they appreciated this. We borrowed company-event themes and made them relevant at the sales team level. We curated what was happening at the macro level of the company for the sales organization. The sales managers provided the leadership in translating corporate goals to actionable, team-level themes. Here are some of the themes we chose:

- Year of the Service Cloud
- Year of the Customer
- Power of You

The theme you come up with will permeate everything you do. The result is magical, and your ROI on the event will be huge.

Gamification at an Event: An Experiment

Given the buzz around gamification technologies and principles, one year we experimented with gamification as a way to drive key learning goals. We used technology to motivate sales teams to act before, during, and after the event. There were some great results and also some good lessons learned about things for us to avoid.

I share this story for sales managers and sales teams who want to embrace gamification. I suspect anything can be gamified, but it's important to prioritize what should be approached in this way. Don't gamify an event or team activity just for the sake of it or because you read a great article. Be deliberate about what you're trying to do.

When we rolled out a sales-kickoff game, our intent was to ensure our sales teams were coming to the event prepared. We issued points and badges for watching product videos and successfully completing tests. We saw a 95 percent completion rate the night before the start of the event. Thus, the pre-event gamification was a huge success.

We created a set of videos that we published to the application. We added questions after each video to make sure our salespeople were absorbing the messages and product training. We created sales assets and videos, spanning all of our product solutions. This was what we called the pre-work. We launched the application and the pre-work on Thursday, five days before the event started.

By Sunday, we had close to 80 percent of the salespeople completing the pre-work, and by the day that the event started on Tuesday, we had close to 95 percent. This was a home run. The comments that were coming in were great; nothing felt forced, and the salespeople were learning. The videos were short and punchy and the quizzes were challenging. Sales management appreciated that they had full visibility of who on their teams completed the pre-work and how they did.

I learned some important lessons during this event. Even with the power of gamification, which I appreciate and respect, sometimes the human aspect can get lost. Even though the game did serve as an icebreaker at the event and did accomplish some of the learning goals, I saw people at the event focusing more on the game rather than looking at the person in front of them to say hello. Don't let yourself get lost in the technology. Keep it human.

Can Virtual Events Be Motivational, Too?

One of the most impactful sales kickoffs I developed in my career was one we ran virtually. We made history, bringing thousands of people together for a sales kickoff via a live video broadcast. No one thought we could energize and educate our teams virtually. Gathering in San Francisco, Dublin, Toronto, Chicago, Atlanta, and New York City, the audience energy was high as they saw the executive team joined by a great lineup of speakers, including sales heroes, top performers, customer champions, and amazing partners. This exciting broadcast enabled participants to see their colleagues live on camera and hear their cheers and success stories.

The power of the virtual kickoff was that the teams were able to dive deep on selling practices that were local to their markets and teams. Keeping events local, with local cultural nuances, allows less time out of the field and away from home. After all, travel is a killer. Avoiding it means that costs are kept way down and funds are freed up to be used for sales programs that have a more quantifiable return on investment. I always partnered with local leaders to give them a voice. The first-line sales manager becomes a much more active leader in the delivery of messages and priorities when events are run locally. I remember spending quality time with the sales leader in one city, helping him prepare for his local sales-kickoff keynote. It was a great opportunity for this person to shine and assert himself as the head of the region.

Certainly there are some challenges that need to be considered with virtual events, but they can all be overcome with technology and the right preplanning.

Integrate Philanthropy into Your Events

I would like to encourage you to consider integrating philanthropy into your business and to have community support be a core value of your sales team. I learned a lot about the power of service from the Salesforce Foundation:

> The Salesforce.com Foundation is based on a simple idea: Leverage Salesforce.com's people, technology, and resources to build collective knowledge and enable action to improve communities throughout the world. We call our integrated philanthropic approach the 1/1/1 model.[22]

To make philanthropy part of your culture, set time aside at your team meeting. Find a local charity that is meaningful to your team. Ask the team and let them nominate organizations for consideration. The impact of bringing the team together under the umbrella of giving back to their community will be huge for morale, camaraderie, and personal satisfaction. You can give back to your communities in so many ways:

1. Pack food and health kits.

2. Work at a local food bank.

3. Volunteer time at a hospital.

4. Paint a school or community center.

5. Clean up outdoor parks or nature reserves.

As the sales manager and leader of the group, the power is in your hands to make this a priority for the team. You can never do enough foundation work, and having this as a part of your team's culture will make a lasting impression on them.

• • •

The power of motivation can never be overestimated. Different types of motivational strategies deliver different value. Gamification is a great motivator that drives active engagement. Incentive travel tends to push salespeople to exceed their goals because of the social pressures of not making the goal. Don't forget the power of a fun, exciting travel-package announcement that arrives at home, motivating the kids to inquire. Philanthropic activity delivers a different kind of motivation that touches on the human spirit. In all cases, special incentive programs designed for sales teams build camaraderie and improve loyalty.

CHAPTER 8

ONBOARD REPS RAPIDLY

The faster and better you hire and onboard new salespeople, the better your bottom line will look. Everyone knows this, but hiring and onboarding still take a backseat to other sales productivity initiatives.

The cost of losing newly hired and onboarded salespeople can run to millions of dollars per person. Onboarding is one of the largest investments a company makes and is also one of the biggest time investments for a sales manager. It should be no surprise that new-hire ramp time is one of the top performance indicators of a successful sales machine. When I work with onboarding teams, I encourage them to embrace a concept called "hire to Hawaii." This phrase has become an onboarding mantra to me because it clarifies the goal of the whole process—you want your new hires to be so successful that they're rewarded with a Hawaii incentive trip in the first year.

The intent of every sales onboarding program is to create many meaningful learning and mentoring experiences that get new hires trained and acclimated more rapidly. The onboarding programs of many sales teams, however, rather than being tightly focused and strategic, are a bit all over the map. What I tend to see are onboarding programs that are all well-intentioned to-do lists and links to content.

A well-thought-out plan with "just in time" content, clear expectation setting, and metrics forms the basis of successful onboarding programs. That said, the real magic of effective onboarding lies in the strength of the sales manager and the rest of the extended team, all of whom accelerate a new hire's training with personalized coaching and mentoring. In this chapter we'll look at the principles of a winning onboarding program and share examples, proven strategies, and a framework for ramping up new hires faster and better. Many companies and sales managers have adopted the framework and philosophies outlined in this chapter to rapidly ramp their sales teams. For many, these onboarding best practices couldn't have come at a better time. I hope they serve you well, too!

Recruitment and hiring does precede the onboarding journey, so we'll start this chapter by diving into some best practices I've seen implemented in this area by winning sales managers.

ALWAYS BE RECRUITING

The best sales managers set hiring targets and always make their hiring numbers. It's an important part of the job, especially in high-growth companies. Sourcing and hiring the best salespeople is best thought of as a core part of a sales manager's business. Use local marketing and networking events to build a pipeline of recruitment prospects and scale the sourcing of new people. Be creative and use social channels like LinkedIn to tap into personal networks and find great candidates.

Successful sales managers have a system for hiring that includes using their teams to help scale the interview process, too. Hiring should, after all, be a team sport. One sales manager I know would have the members of his sales team all participate in the hiring process. This sales manager would space out the interviews with the recruits and hold them at different times of the day to get a sense of the salesperson's comfort level and etiquette at breakfast, lunch, and dinner. I won't share the stories that I heard, but you can imagine what you learn about someone by watching them in a social setting such as eating a meal at a restaurant. The interviewees then reported back what they observed and experienced, providing another hiring decision criterion.

Another great hiring best practice is to have the applicant deliver a pitch in front of a panel of their potential peers and other executives. It's a great way to involve everyone in the process and to see how the applicant performs on his or her feet. Here's a simple way to employ this strategy: Provide a prospect with a company scenario and a simple set of your company slides. Have them prepare, and set the expectation that they are coming in for a presentation—but don't give them all the answers. The good ones will do their homework and customize the presentation. Look to see if they are adding things like an agenda, next steps, and references to the presentation. Check to see how resourceful they are. It should be pretty easy for them to go to your website and find some customer stories they can inject into a standard presentation. See how much discovery they push for before the call and what kind of information they are interested in finding out. If they are customer-minded by nature, it will show in how and what they present. Once the prospect's presentation is over, solicit opinions from your entire team. Establish a sales profile to create a recruiting scorecard. Make the scorecard available to candidates and the interviewing team. Having a scorecard will help create alignment.

ONBOARDING PRINCIPLES

At salesforce.com, we invested a lot of time, resources, and technology to make the new-hire journey successful. Over the years, my team ran over seventy boot camp programs and onboarded thousands of customer-facing sales employees and partners. In that time, we revamped the boot camp program many times, always innovating as we went and seeking to make it better, even though we consistently scored high and always received amazing feedback. Given the rate of change and growth, we needed to be ahead of the curve.

The result was that our boot camp program evolved a lot over the years. It went from two weeks to five days and then back up to eight days. It morphed from a one-size-fits-all program to include role-based days to meet the unique needs of different sales segments. This change reflected the fact that, for example, inside sellers and enterprise sellers are very different in how they sell and thus in how they need to be onboarded. We also focused on incorporating as much hands-on experience as we could in the boot camp workshops and encouraged social learning wherever possible.

After creating so many amazing onboarding experiences for thousands of new hires at salesforce.com, there are definitely things we did well and some things we always found ourselves improving. The task of running many onboarding programs became an exercise in being creative; we tried to get away from "death by PowerPoint" and move toward more active learning.

One year, we decided to convert all the content presented in boot camp to self-paced learning with periodic "knowledge checks" to make sure participants were grasping the material. This enabled us to rethink our boot camp experience and create an opportunity for more social learning, networking, and hands-on exercises. Many presentations that had been delivered by product managers in the old boot camp format could be easily converted to video presentations. This made room for a collaborative, case-study approach that was more common in boot camp programs. Our alignment with marketing helped make this happen. In this way, the product managers are still engaged in the onboarding and boot-camp programs, but their level of engagement is different. In this new world, product managers and executives came in with a more conversational style, ready to answer questions live.

For those of you starting from scratch, recognize the opportunity to create active learning and mentoring for your new hires from the very beginning. Resist the urge to create a static list of learning objectives and materials that you hand off to your new hire with little more than some booklets and a few links to videos to watch. Put yourself in their shoes. Whether you have one or one hundred new people starting, think of each one as being your first and only employee. Create something special for them that is personalized and that ties directly to the learning they need to excel in the job. If you make the leap to an interactive learning experience, you'll have a much better chance of having every one of your new hires exceeding quota and sitting on the beach in Hawaii in his or her first year.

As you create your onboarding materials, partner with your colleagues in marketing; they will have a lot of assets you can leverage. Ask them to rate your current program, and encourage their input. The key is not to overwhelm the new hires, but to curate the right content for your sales teams. If you have a sales enablement team in place, then work closely with them. They will likely oversee the global onboarding program and will work with you to make your process amazing.

As you build your program, make sure that it's tailored to give trainees information when they need it. Don't train them on how to process an order on the first day if you have a ninety-day sales cycle and they won't be processing orders until much later. Ease them into your culture by focusing on the skills they will need in the short term. Have them meet people and be a sponge in their first days.

Like hiring—and so much else a sales team does—onboarding is a group activity. Build a culture of mentorship. Using the foundations from your team assessment, you can identify mentors who are subject-matter experts to help onboard new members to your sales team. If you are in a larger organization, partner up with other sales managers and do cross-team mentoring. There is nothing more powerful than a salesperson who has experience in a certain domain, sharing their experiences with new hires. I'll say it again: Salespeople learn from other salespeople, and they appreciate instruction that's based on real-life experiences.

Finally, make the onboarding experience fun.

CREATE YOUR OWN ONBOARDING PROGRAM

It *is* within your reach to build an onboarding program for your new salespeople that borrows elements from enterprise companies yet still has a local, personalized impact—even if you don't have many resources to devote to it. As a sales manager, you know your team and your market best. You also know what resources you can expect from headquarters, so planning properly will improve the effectiveness of your program.

I was recently working with a young, hot, energetic start-up, and at one point I met with the head of sales, their sales managers, and their sales operations leader. We talked about their sales-productivity challenges and specifically their onboarding goals. The head of sales shared that he felt his company was ready for an enterprise-class onboarding program. With that, we had our marching orders, and we went straight to work.

Assess What You Have

It didn't take us long to assess the program they had in place and restructure it in a way that would prepare them for their upcoming waves of hiring. After clarifying goals and aligning on tactics, we put an action plan in place.

We started by taking an inventory of all the great assets they already had. Like many companies, their list of onboarding links and assets were spread across a variety of websites, intranets, and video servers. We found links to webinars, customer videos on YouTube, internal videos, playbooks, and many more presentations. The good news was that this company had a lot of high-value assets in place, so a best practice onboarding framework mixed with a layer of peer-to-peer mentoring and a lot of accountability would go a long way.

Organize and Categorize

Once we completed this task, we quickly began organizing everything across a set of categories. The categorization of all the assets created a platform for us to evolve their old onboarding into a world-class experience for their new hires. We were disciplined about rating each piece of content and then marking it as either suitable for pre-work, workshop (a.k.a. boot camp), or mentorship. Each piece of content was mapped to a set of learning pillars: culture, product, industry, competitiveness, sales skills, and sales process. We accomplished the inventory, ratings, and the mapping in a two-hour working session with a big whiteboard and a lot of open-minded creativity. It was a collaborative effort between sales operations and the sales managers. We also brought in marketing to contribute to the process, after a new baseline program had been established.

The content was then placed into a master thirty-day schedule that became the foundation of this company's onboarding program.

From this work we also derived a set of key metrics to be shared with sales management and every new salesperson. Besides updating the content and presenting it in a much more organized way, we created more transparency and accountability. Each sales manager using the program knew what his or her role was within the region and how to leverage this great work to augment what was already happening. The partnership between sales management, sales operations, and marketing made the creation of this new onboarding program a huge success.

When we ran this working session together, we asked ourselves a few questions to maximize learning impact and onboarding success:

1. Is this content best consumed individually or in a group setting?
2. When should this content be introduced?
3. How will we measure learning and effectiveness of each piece of content?

Define Onboarding Roles

We aimed to strike the right balance between self-paced, pre-work learning, hands-on exercises for a boot camp, and mentoring that would happen after boot camp. We assigned clear roles; we defined who was doing what, and expectations were set for early performance measures based on the learning goals.

At the end of every week, the salesperson and the sales manager were clear on goals and deliverables. At the end of the first week of this new program, after watching the videos, reading materials, and partnering with other salespeople for mentorship, a salesperson would be expected to complete a knowledge check, a hybrid between a test and an in-person meeting with the sales manager. The conversation was structured and based on the week's work. There were no surprises. I've seen this model work, and in some cases sales managers will nominate a mentor from their team each week who will be available to answer questions and inform the team about how the new hire is doing.

FIRST THIRTY DAYS

As the person accountable for your new hires' success, you must own this process. Your sales productivity and operations teams can partner with marketing and enlist their help in creating templates. Hopefully, these teams can provide you with an onboarding framework you can then personalize, adapting it to the individual needs of your new sales rep hires.

As you think about what you want the experience to be for your new salesperson, remember to balance self-paced learning, workshops, and peer mentorship. Prescribe the right learning at the right time and make sure to include your learning pillars. Make the calendar known from day one, and make it visible to your entire team so they can assist in the onboarding too.

Warm Welcome Letter

Let's now walk through the thirty-day onboarding experience. First impressions are everything, so start with a welcome letter— or welcome video—to the new hire from your top sales leader or CEO. The welcome should be warm and sincere and should make this person feel excited to be a part of the company and its culture. When I became a citizen of the United States, in my "onboarding" package was a personal letter from the president welcoming me to the American family; it felt amazing to receive that letter, and that's the feeling you want to create in the new hire.

	Monday	Tuesday	Wednesday	Thursday	Friday
Week 1 (Self-Paced Pre-work & Team Huddles)	Company & Culture	Products	Competitive	Customer Stories	Certification Prep
	Mentorship (One-on-ones with team & daily check-ins)				
Week 2 (Boot camp Workshop)	Travel Day	Executive Welcome Workshop & Networking	Case Study Team Exercise	Case Study Competition	Pre-work Prep & Test
				Sales Process Workshop	Pitch Certification
				Certification Prep	
Week 3 (Field Readiness)	Team-Building Evening Events				
		Social Prospecting	Prospecting Outreach		Territory Planning & Readiness Certification
	Mentorship (One-on-ones with team)				
	Compelling Events	Discovery Questions	Value-Based Discovery		
Week 4 (Building Pipeline & Closing Business)	Sales Process				
	Daily Check-In				Pipeline & Deal Review
	Self-paced	Certification	Workshop	Mentorship	

Pre-work

After the welcome message, shift right into pre-work—the background work that will prepare the new hire for boot camp. In the pre-work part of onboarding, starting on the very first day, they'll learn the basics of the product, the sales process, the customer base, the competition, the culture of the company and team, and what will be expected of them. At salesforce.com, we created pre-work videos that covered topics spanning the learning pillars of culture, product, sales execution, and "do my job" training. Consider creating a video library to serve as the core of pre-work. Such a pre-work library should provide the trainee with more than twenty hours of learning time, including fun exercises and daily check-ins. Enlist as many executives and management colleagues as possible to help create and deliver pre-work onboarding videos. This is a great way to let the new hire get acquainted with top leaders in the organization. Today's technology makes it easy to create high-quality videos that fit into an overall onboarding strategy. If you're not able to create the video library, then create a pre-work agenda with the same topics and keep the new hire on a schedule with meetings and mentorship.

Boot-camp Workshop

After all the pre-work has been completed and a knowledge check is measured with a test or a coaching interview at the end of the first week, the new hire is eligible to join a boot camp learning experience. Some companies will have a formal boot camp learning program and others won't. If you're starting from scratch, then this chapter will be a great guide to help you build something that will help you onboard your new hires faster and better. If you're a sales manager without a formal onboarding program, you're empowered to create your own. Many sales managers I worked with at salesforce.com, even with an amazing and well-respected onboarding program, still had their own program mapped to the unique skills of the new salesperson and the local market conditions. The key is to focus on the salesperson experience and make sure what happens locally complements what might happen in the headquarters boot camp program.

The boot camp program at salesforce.com is one of the best on the planet; it consists of a very intense headquarters-based eight-day workshop that assumes the pre-work has been success-fully completed. Over the years, the boot camp classes ranged from ten to fifteen salespeople to up to more than one hundred per boot camp. Attendance varied with recruiting cycles and goals, including seasonality and economic conditions. Here are some tips to keep your boot camp experience engaging. Fill your boot camp agenda with a lot of team selling exercises, including a case-study simula-tion. Make it fun, too: Sprinkle social events throughout to keep the energy levels high and to let trainees get to know everyone. Alternate evenings between networking events led by teams from headquarters and working sessions intended to prepare trainees for the next day of boot camp. Even from the beginning, prepare new hires to always win as a team and to inject a team spirit that's so crucial to high performance.

I was inspired by Tony Robbins to think of an icebreaker any company can easily make happen at the beginning of boot camp to emphasize the importance of thinking big and using storytell-ing to build relationships with customers. On day one of a boot camp experience, I would recommend having each person at the workshop spend a few minutes writing down his or her own career story and then present it to the person sitting next to them. Then have a few volunteers share their stories with the entire room. These career stories are always remarkable, and the whole team benefits from getting to know each other. As part two of the icebreaker, I would have all the trainees write down the story of their future: "What will your story be," I asked, "after you've achieved unprecedented success in your new career?" The power of self-actualization is very motivational and so is the power of sharing, which is what makes this icebreaker so effective. Incor-porate these kinds of collaborative, social, inspirational exercises as often as possible as you construct your own boot camp.

To help the new hires and the onboarding team stay focused

on the right objectives, give each day in boot camp a theme. Consider creating, for example, culture days, product days, or case-study days.

Coaching and Mentoring on the Job

After the boot camp experience, which happens somewhere in the third week of the first thirty days, the sales teams return home to their locations. Sales managers in regions are there to help salespeople integrate all the learning and best practices with their territories and day-to-day activities. Your objective, when the new hires head home after a training experience at headquarters, is to have established a strong enough foundation during the pre-work sessions that they'll feel like they're coming home—returning from an expertly arranged trip and arriving back at a place where someone is waiting for them.

After the sales teams are back in their offices in their home regions, the last part of the first thirty days is a personalized onboarding plan designed and ready for them to use in their territories. Now that they've gone through welcoming, pre-work, and boot camp, it's time for the local sales team and sales manager to start integrating the new hire into the coaching and training programs you already have in place for the rest of the team.

MONITOR AND MEASURE EARLY INDICATORS

Every business owner must ensure that each of his or her assets is at full capacity and providing a great return on investment. The challenge of onboarding salespeople is no different. Sales managers should manage the productivity of new sales hires across key metrics and deliverables. Rather than waiting until the end of the year or some time in the far-off future to see how your new hires are performing, start measuring them early. Every business and industry will have its own set of indicators as to how a salesperson is performing. The important thing is to identify the behaviors that can forecast the likelihood of a salesperson's success—and to do it early. One of the big benefits of creating a structured onboarding program is the opportunity to watch for early indicators. Look for successful completion of the pre-work videos and tests; watch for participation in the boot camp case-study simulation. Make sure all new hires can successfully deliver the first-call pitch and other must-know presentations.

In the technology space, it's very common to measure a salesperson's ability to deliver a sales pitch that includes a technical demonstration. Every technology company I encounter makes it clear to salespeople that they need to come to boot camp prepared to deliver the company's first-call presentation along with a technical demonstration. In order to spice it up and add a bit of competitiveness, the salespeople are also warned that they could be called on during the workshop to stand and deliver the presentation in front of the new-hire class. I have seen this practice also come to life in the field by sales managers. They'll have the new hire present the presentation to the entire team days or weeks after they start. It's a rite of passage for some. Having newly hired salespeople stand and deliver a presentation and demonstration is a great way to get early indicators around strengths and weaknesses that can inform a sales coaching program early in a career.

• • •

The sales managers who have teams that are all successful provide clarity around activity. To provide this clarity is to align everyone on a common set of goals. With onboarding, being clear about what new hires should be accomplishing every week and how they will be measured is a powerful way to motivate sales teams from day one. Make it fun, interactive, and memorable—and remember, avoid death by PowerPoint.

EXECUTION

CHAPTER 9

OWN YOUR SALES PROCESS

Your sales teams will appreciate a sales process that you use and respect. How can *you* expect your sales team to embrace and adopt a way of selling that you have not integrated with your sales-management practice? It starts at the top and it is up to you to lead by example. Show your sales team how you use your sales system and how you depend on your sales process to manage the business.

As a sales manager, you are best positioned to operationalize the sales process through your cadence and daily reinforcement. A customer-focused sales process, when documented thoughtfully and thoroughly, becomes part of your sales culture. It guides the rhythm of your business and officiates a sales-execution discipline. It helps you scale sales best practices. It forms the foundation of every deal and customer conversation.

A winning sales process should be real and actionable. You know you have a winning sales process when it truly becomes a salesperson's everyday tool. It complements what salespeople know and how they already sell. A well-adopted sales process gives sales teams that extra push to accelerate sales performance. As the CEO of your business, it is up to you to set the right expectations around reporting cadence and updating deal information. The sales process provides you with that tool to distribute ownership and account-ability across the team.

It's likely that a sales process—and maybe even a formal sales methodology—is already in place for you or your company. This chapter is not a discussion of the pros and cons of the different sales methodologies available. They are all great and you should not underestimate the value of an "out of the box" solution, many of which—like Target Account Selling (TAS) Group's—have decades' worth of best practices behind them, along with very nice integra-tions with CRM applications like Salesforce.

But that doesn't mean that you can coast along and rely solely on a sales process designed by someone else. Your team has unique needs, and even the most powerful of proprietary sales processes must be transformed to become part of your team's culture—to fit *your* reps, *your* product, *your* industry. In this chapter, we're going to look at the fundamentals of a winning sales process, whether you're working with an existing model or building one from scratch. It's up to you to own your sales process and bring it to life in your deals. After all, you're on the hook for the team's target—you and no one else.

THE SALES PROCESS AND YOU

As a sales manager, there are a few scenarios in front of you as you read this chapter.

First, you could be a sales manager working for a big company. If so, the company likely has a sales process already in place. It's your job to own the sales process and to reinforce it with your sales team and in your deals. You'll want to understand how the sales process fits in with forecasting. You will want to use the information uncovered in the sales process by your sales teams to apply judgment to the forecast submitted by your sales team. You'll want to employ the principles in your sales process to coaching, mentoring, and deal reviews. This chapter will help you understand how to personalize the sales process to your style and to your sales team's go-to market.

Second, you may be one of the first or perhaps the very first sales manager in your company. In that case, it could be that the company does not have a documented sales process, and it's your job to help create one. It's great to see so many sales managers I worked with now leading sales teams of start-ups and tasked with creating their own sales cultures and supporting sales processes. They truly understand the power of ownership and personalization of the sales process, as many have reached out to me asking for help and guidance in creating their own versions of the SUCCESS formula and the sales process we created at salesforce.com. Regardless of what industry you are in, creating a strong sales process will accelerate your team's performance. The sales process, coupled with the sales values, will be foundational to creating consistency and discipline in your team.

A third scenario is you have been asked to join a task force led by sales operations to refresh the company's sales process. Your involvement will be instrumental in creating a sales process that reflects the reality of what's going on in deals and in the field. Use this chapter to come prepared with best practices. Share it with the project team and be ready to share your real-life experiences with the extended team.

There are many books, blogs, and manuals on creating a winning sales process, but I'll cut out all the noise for you and share some tools you can apply immediately to your business.

MANAGE WHAT YOU MEASURE

Peter Drucker—an educator, author, and strategist and one of the foremost philosophical and practical contributors to the disciplines of management and the modern corporation—is often quoted as saying, "You can't manage what you can't measure." This principle applies to the world of sales. The foundation of measuring sales results is rooted in a well-defined sales process that is understood and adopted by sales teams. Bring the sales process into your management cadence and make it seamless to your sales teams. Be the sales manager that lives in your sales system and not in a spreadsheet and you will experience tremendous benefits.

Identifying, documenting, and sharing your company's sales process with your sales teams and partners will have a dramatic impact on your bottom line. Mapping your sales process to your customer's buying process is equally if not more important. As a sales manager, being transparent about what customer information needs to be discovered and answered during sales engagements brings the sales process to life. The data fields that live in a sales system should map back to actionable behavior sales teams do in their day-to-day sales activity and with every customer interaction. It forms the foundation for a common language across the sales team. Aligning your sales teams around what they do and what information you need from them is a very important piece of the sales productivity formula.

If you subscribe to this philosophy, you are well on your way to amazing results. Deal velocity will be faster. Win rates will be higher. You will find salespeople ramping quicker. Salespeople will be more accomplished. Pipeline quality will improve. Forecasting judgment will be better. All in all, you will have a much stronger and more productive sales organization—if you measure what you manage. As mentioned in chapter 2, the focus and innovation represented by creating sales values and bringing them to life in a sales process will drive home how to get deals done. Your success is grounded in a team playbook that maps back to a sales process that is reinforced in weekly team meetings.

There are some very important lessons that I want to make sure you take advantage of in order to energize and analyze your sales process. Equally if not more important than the actual sales process are the reports that are based on the sales process to measure team performance. Make sure you are focused on activity, pipeline, and revenue metrics. Here are some tips to remember as you energize your own sales process.

First, be very clear about what is being measured. Set the expectation from day one. Share a sample report with the actual metrics to avoid any confusion. The best sales managers are transparent about what is most important. Rather than send out a PowerPoint presentation or an Excel spreadsheet, send a link to a report from your sales system. If you do not, then why should your sales team use your sales system to update their deals? It's a vicious circle that starts with you, the sales manager. If the reports do not exist, then create them. If you cannot create the reports, then look for help. Be direct about how the sales process impacts forecasting and pipeline quality.

Second, be consistent about what you measure. Use the same metrics and key performance indicators on your weekly team meetings and quarterly business reviews. If you change any assumptions, then reset the expectation and be ready to explain why.

Third, do not forget to have the reports ready to go before you launch a new sales process to your sales teams. I remember rolling out a new sales process one year, and the missing ingredient was reports for the first-line sales managers to reinforce expectations and actions with every sales team.

BUILD A PROFILE OF A WINNING DEAL

Regardless of where you are in the sales organizational hierarchy, building the archetype of a winning deal is a great use of your time. Winning sales processes are born from the heart and soul of a company. The most adopted sales processes are the ones that your sales community plays a part in creating from conversations and interviews with top performers, sales leaders, and customers. Ideas and best practices should come from every member of the extended team, including sales engineers, product managers, technical specialists, and partners.

Documenting how and why your sales team wins deals will pay huge dividends. I urge every company I talk to about optimizing their sales process to invest sufficient time in knowing this in detail. If you want to model the best behaviors and scale your business, have your sales team share exactly what worked at every step in their winning sales cycles. Look for their "aha!" moments and document them so that you can scale their successes across the rest of your sales team.

These interviews should be conducted with an open mind. Don't make any assumptions, and remember the power of curiosity. Typically, when I interview a sales team, I start at the beginning and have them walk me through the entire sales cycle:

- Where did the lead come from?
- How was the prospect qualified?
- What business problems were being solved?
- What were the buyer's personal and economic drivers?
- How quickly did the sales team uncover the compelling event?
- How was value positioned?

These questions and many others help identify the character-istics of a good sales process. Use them as a baseline for your deal interviews, and also as a baseline for your sales process. As you go through the questions, ask your team for examples of meetings—notes and customer conversations. The more real and detailed the answers become, the more real the sales process will be to sales teams—and the more it will be accepted by them. Take time to go through the entire story. Collect any and all emails and sales tools used in the sales cycle by the sales team. These can become best practice assets for other salespeople to use in their sales cycles.

As you continue your interview with the sales team, your next step is to understand how much time was spent on discovery and what was uncovered. Ask for a list of the discovery questions that were used to prepare for the meeting, and collect any notes docu-mented. These might be in a sales system or they might live in an email folder or in the mind of the salesperson. It really doesn't matter where the information is as long as you get access to the detail. Find out all the stakeholders who were involved in the discovery phase. Try to understand why the customer made a buy decision based on what was learned during the discovery phases. Being able to trend best practices of how sales teams engage with customers in the early stages of a sales process does a lot to improve pipeline quality. I was working with one sales team and we uncovered that asking about a top executive's priority early on was the key to driving urgency in deals and keeping the entire sales team and all stakeholders aligned on a shared goal. We turned this realization into sales process email alerts that were automatically sent out seven days after an opportunity was cre-ated to remind salespeople to get to power and understand their top priorities.

Besides the business problem and the technical discovery, find out what was learned about the decision-making process and the evaluation criteria, too. A lot of clues about customer buying motivations can be uncovered by finding out why certain criteria were established and why they were important. Collect all presentations shared with customers, as these winning presentations are great tools that can be used in future deals for other members of your sales team. I consider customized presentations created by salespeople to be gold—especially those that result in closed business.

Leave room at the end of the interview for a free-form dialogue, allowing the sales team to talk through what worked and what didn't work in the sales cycle.

DESIGN YOUR PROCESS

Once you've done all your research interviews and observation, designing the sales process should not be hard; you have already done all the heavy lifting. You're ready to channel your sales values and your research into a sales process that makes sense for your sales teams. Here are the elements that you should include in the sales process: forecast stages, sales stages, sales stage exit criteria, and supporting sales tools. On the next page is a template you can use as a starting point, which has worked for many colleagues and companies alike. Less is more for an exercise like this.

The top line shows the sales stages in order from one to six. The rows underneath represent the activities or tasks that a sales team needs to accomplish to move between stages. Use this as a starting point, but don't hesitate to alter this to fit the particular needs of your team, your product, and your customers. Partner with members of the sales operations and sales strategy groups to help officiate your sales process and bring it to life.

1. Prospect	2. Qualify	3. Demonstrate	4. Validate	5. Negotiate	6. Close
I've identified	I've determined	I've shared	I've validated	I've secured	I've received
Business Issues	Compelling Event	Demonstration to Buyers and Influencers	Business Case and ROI	Internal Approval & Delivered Proposal	Written Confirm by Customer
Business Impact	Decision-Making Process and Evaluation Criteria	Customer References & Stories	Customer Success Plan (Close Plan)	Project Implementation Plan	Customer PO and Signatures Received
Budget	Decision Makers, Influencers, and Sponsors	Customer Success Plan (Close Plan)	No Roadblocks or Red Flags	Pricing and Contract Terms Agreed to by Customer	

CUSTOMIZE YOUR SALES PROCESS

The goal of customization and personalization is to help your sales teams master the sales process and be more productive every moment of the day.

Your goal is to codify your sales process and then to bring it to life in your sales system. You want your sales teams to work and live in your sales application. You want them to prepare, present, follow up, and do all their reporting in your sales system. To do this you need to make the experience model how they run their business and how they sell.

I have audited companies' sales processes and taken a look at their main sales entry pages, and I've discovered that sometimes the page looks like a form designed for sales operations or even finance. I have seen pages that prioritize the "order to cash" part of the sales process and do not focus on the stages leading up to the order. If your sales pages have way too many data fields and are not organized in a thoughtful way, putting the salesperson use case first, then you have some work to do.

I recommend building sections on your main sales page that map to your sales process and your sales stages. I work with companies all the time to create sections on the sales page that correlate with the core selling values. It's a simple thing to do in most sales systems but goes a long way to help salespeople visualize what they should do and when they should do it. Each one of sales activities can be much more integrated with your team's day-to-day activities if they are properly organized and displayed in your sales system. The presentation, simplicity, and priority of these fields on the sales entry form make the biggest difference. Company after company, the conversation is always the same. We take a look at their sales pages in their sales automation systems. We net out what fields are most important and then remove the rest. There is no need for confusion and extra noise.

Included here is a sample best practice sales page used by sales teams. It represents an amalgamation of all the generic, nonproprietary best practices. What people like most about this page is the way it's organized: the sequence of the fields and the page's

Deal Info

Opportunity Name	CRM Solution Project	Opportunity Owner	Elay Cohen
Account Name	ABC Manufacturer	Amount	$150, 000.00
Type	New Business	Close Date	6/30/2013
Forecast Category	Best Case	Stage	Proposal Price Quote
Quote Delivered	✓	Probability (%)	75%
Deal Source	Partner registered deal	Closing Countdown	184.00

Sales Criteria

Challenges	Increase revenues, grow customer base, open new markets	Budgeted	✓
Compelling Event	Annual Sales Kickoff	Proposal submitted	✓
User stories	Sales force automation, channel managment, social selling	Executive Champion	Amy Smith
Business Case	300% ROI in Year 1	Decision Role	Chief Sales Officer
Decision-making Process	Board level approval	Next Step	Review contract terms
Customer References	Hardware Company VP Sales Furniture Company Director Sales OPS Sales Effectiveness	Mutual Close Plan	1. Demo sign off 2. Build Proposal 3. Create implementation blueprint 4. Meet procurement requests 5. Board level sign off 6. Get PO

Competition

Competitor	XYZ	Competitive Status	Ahead
Competitive Strategy	Use XYZ Playbook	Competitive Deal	✓

cleanliness. The page is uncluttered. As you look to clean up your sales system, remove any fields that are not used anymore and institute a governance model restricting adding fields to a small decision-making body.

Take a moment to see how the page is organized. The focus of the page is the sales criteria that tie back to sales values. All of the fields become questions that a sales manager can ask a salesperson during a deal review or a forecast call.

SALES VALUES TO INFORM SALES PROCESS

There should be a clear correlation between values and expectations. If there isn't, you have some work to do. Say one of your sales values is "Uncover customer's pain." If that's the case, your sales process needs to clearly establish *how* reps are expected to do that. I suggest creating questions, inputs, and tools that live inside your sales system to help salespeople uncover critical business issues through thoughtful discovery.

The products and services offered by companies in Silicon Valley enamor many salespeople. Some salespeople, as soon as they get the first scent of a customer business problem, are quick to the draw with a pitch or a demonstration. They shift from listening to talking. They are not solving problems; they are selling products. In order to fix this, a sales manager would create a sales value like "Uncover customer's pain" or "Be curious." The sales manager would then ensure that these values came to life in the sales process and were reinforced in team sales huddles. For example, the salesperson would be reminded that he couldn't move from step 2 to step 3 until a complete and thoughtful discovery was completed, with supporting documentation in place demonstrating that he understood the true pain of the customer. Data fields would need to be completed and filled in by the salesperson or through some automated way based on email activity or tasks completed. The sales manager would be able to call on these fields to check on status in weekly sales huddles. The importance of the fields would be displayed in reports used by the sales manager. Values need to connect with the sales process and with the reports used by sales managers to be fully operationalized and effective.

Here is another example showing how to connect a core sales value with a sales process with the intent to drive a set of behaviors by your reps. If "customer storytelling" were a sales value of your team, you would identify when in the sales process you wanted to trigger your people to start sharing customer stories and sales references. I suggest having every salesperson share customer stories and examples from the very beginning of the customer buying experience. You could use the sales process to share relevant customer stories with your sales team at different times of the sales campaign. Imagine you are a salesperson and you have a deal you're working for a company in a specific industry—what if a set of relevant customer stories and references were pushed to you right before a customer meeting? That seems like a compelling way to add value to the sales process.

CROWDSOURCE AND BUILD YOUR PLAYBOOK

The next step is to build product or selling playbooks that go a level deeper than a sales process. A playbook contains the documentation and best practices of how you sell. Sales playbooks are best when they are informed by winning strategies, tactics, and tools that have worked well for salespeople. Crowdsourcing sales teams for what they have created or customized is the secret sauce of a winning sales playbook. I have seen teams, including my own, spin many cycles trying to create sales playbooks. My goal here is to help you avoid spinning cycles by giving you a best practice sales playbook template that you can implement immediately. There might be nuances that are unique to your business, but sharing this with your teams will get you started and save you months of meetings.

The most successful sales managers always maintain their own specific playbooks tailored to their geography or industry. Smart marketers will tap into the energy and best practices that live with first-line sales managers and their teams. Warning: It's a recipe for disaster to assume that once you develop your core selling playbook you are done. The best sales managers are always iterating their sales playbooks based on changing market conditions and new competitors. Here are the components of a best practice sales playbook that I have seen work for sales teams. You can use these elements as a starting point to create a playbook tailored to your business.

1. What's in It for Me?

Grab the attention of your salespeople and answer the fundamental question: What is in it for them? Why should they care? How will they make money? How will they grow their deals? Partner with marketing or your sales operations team to collate this information if it's not readily available to you.

2. Elevator Pitch

Provide a clear, concise elevator pitch that is natural for your salespeople to present. Have your salespeople share what they use, and create one that is customized by your salespeople themselves. Or use the marketing elevator pitch as a baseline, and then have your teams personalize it.

3. Product and Solutions Overview

Include detail on what you sell, including product-feature sheets, specifications, and solution maps. Take what you can from marketing and your product teams and rely on your teams to personalize the solution and benefit statements.

4. Buyer Profile

Providing your sales team with a detailed discussion about buyer priorities and challenges removes the guesswork. Detail who the audience is and what is important to them. Use specific examples and names of people representing buyers that you have sold to. Provide answers to questions like: What does this buyer care about? How do they measure success? Map challenges to buyers, be specific, and keep it real.

5. Discovery Questions

Providing a list of discovery questions is good and always a top request of salespeople. Even though every discovery call is unique to the customer, you should still have your team build a list of questions together. Crowdsourcing the team for their best questions is a way to make this part of the playbook even more powerful.

6. Objection Handling

Document objections and provide answers to them. Record the most common objection-handling conversations. Map them to the steps in the sales process. Keep the objections and how to handle them current and fresh.

7. Customer Stories and References

Every sales team needs a list of sales references and typical customer stories. Depending on where you are and whom you sell to, you'll need industry-specific stories. Make sure this important asset is part of your sales team's arsenal.

8. Competition

List out your competitors. For each competitor in each segment, include a competitive summary including strengths, weaknesses, opportunities, and threats (SWOT). Be honest and provide real insight into how your competitors are selling against you.

9. Resources

Include a full list of all the available resources that are local and those provided by headquarters. As the sales manager, you have the relationships with folks outside of your team that you can bring in when necessary. Remember the power of winning as a team and the need to nurture internal and external relationships.

● ● ●

Every sales manager should have her own sales playbook that becomes meshed with the company's sales process. In some cases they are one and the same. The playbook defines how every rep on your team is going to go about the day-to-day business of creating, maturing, and closing new business. The sales process brings everyone together around a common set of actions that lead to the desired outcome: more sales.

• • •

Bringing your sales process to life is such an important lever to drive consistency, best practice sharing, and forecast accuracy. The reason you customize your sales process is to improve your judgment on the forecast submitted by your sales team. The sales process includes best practice activity and key information required to be collected at the appropriate sales stage. A customized sales process will help you create pipeline and forecasting reports to use every day in your business instead of living in the world of spreadsheets.

Finally, crowdsourcing winning plays and sales tools will bring your sales values and sales process to life by making your sales team part of its creation. They will engage and adapt if you follow these suggestions.

CHAPTER 10

BUILD QUALIFIED PIPELINE

When I sit down and talk to companies about their sales teams' performance, one of the first things I do is ask the sales manager a question: What are the biggest problems you and your team are facing today? What's keeping you from making—or even better, blowing out—your numbers?

Usually an overwhelmed look comes across the sales manager's face and I begin to hear the team's issues. The session becomes therapeutic as sales managers offload what's going on in their businesses. After listening for a bit, I try to sort their problems into something I can help them take action on immediately.

"Tell me this," I say. "Do you need to empower your salespeople to build more qualified sales pipeline, or are your deals taking too long to close?" The answer to the question quickly points me in the right direction. For example, if they don't have enough deals in their pipeline, I know it's time to talk about *prospecting*—the subject of this chapter. If their deals are getting stuck somewhere in the process, we need to talk about *driving urgency and velocity in deals through more discovery* (covered in the next chapter). I know this seems simplistic, but it helps anchor sales management conversations around core problems.

If the trouble is with prospecting, we need to get to work right away: A steady influx of prospects is the lifeblood of your team and the whole organization. Sales managers help their sales teams create prospecting strategies to build a healthy pipeline and a stream of qualified opportunities. The best salespeople are the ones who appreciate leads that come from marketing but recognize that nothing replaces the hard work of generating their own leads. The most qualified pipeline is always the one created by the salespeople themselves. The best leads are those generated by your team—and it's your job to show them how to get those qualified opportunities in the pipeline. Coaching your team on prospecting and managing and measuring the whole process is the key to building a rich territory, and this chapter will give you the tools you need to do just that. You will help your sales teams prospect better, conduct smarter research, and build prospecting conversations that engage potential customers.

SEE RESULTS WHEN YOU PRIORITIZE PROSPECTING

Every one of your salespeople should have a prospecting strategy. They should each understand the tools available to research executives, companies, and brands. They should know how to convert research into buyer priorities. In short, every salesperson should be an expert in building his or her own pipeline. And it's your job to constantly remind them of the importance of pipeline building. I would even take it a step further and say that it's your job to help your sales teams keep pipeline generation top-of-mind. The only way to do that is to have it be part of the rhythm of your business. Set activity targets, defined by number of emails, calls, and "customer connects" made, along with pipeline targets. A "customer connect" is defined as any interaction with a prospect, whether it's a reply email, a voicemail, or an actual live conversation. Build reports and dashboards to track the pipeline activity of your sales teams, and share their performance broadly. Celebrate successes and highlight best practice activity you want to see emulated from one salesperson to the next.

I have worked with many sales teams and companies over the years to help build new pipeline and drive up pipeline conversion. I have also hired companies specializing in prospecting to help develop a team's email and voicemail skills and increase salespeople's confidence and the company's revenues. I have seen some prospecting campaigns that work, and plenty that don't. I've thought a lot about the common elements of the ones that do, and this chapter captures those thoughts and experiences.

I've shared this framework with many sales teams and have seen some fantastic results, including one company that was prospecting so effectively that it began receiving a flood of connection invitations on LinkedIn from the very prospects they were reaching out to—the customers were reaching out because they considered them subject-matter experts! At the end of the day, salespeople want to be strategic and want to help solve their customers' problems; you just need to help empower them to do this.

From a sales management perspective, you'll want to make prospecting a part of the culture of the team. There are ways to highlight the importance of prospecting with your sales teams. Mark your team calendar with prospecting days. Schedule prospecting sales huddles. Set prospecting goals for the team that trickle down to every salesperson. The responsibility of getting your reps excited about prospecting is all yours.

Not long ago, I was working with a sales manager at a start-up in San Francisco. Our main project: Build more qualified pipeline fast. In the first meeting with the team, we started by covering some prospecting best practices, with a focus on social media and email. The reps all seemed to get it. They were excited, and nearly everyone jumped in with ideas for a new prospecting email template best practice for the team. We all left the meeting energized and optimistic.

Fast-forward two weeks, and I'm on the phone with the sales manager. "How are things going?" I asked, hoping to hear that her unit's pipeline was already benefiting from the recent session.

"Well, pretty slow, actually," she said, sounding a little dejected.

It was disappointing, but I encouraged her to keep at it. I explained that if she wanted pipeline to grow, *she* would have to take charge and constantly *reinforce* how important the team's new prospecting strategy was.

In our next session with the whole team, the sales manager stepped up to the plate and led the discussion by reinforcing the team's prospecting goals. She talked about how pipeline building would become the center of the team's weekly meeting. She emphasized how great the new strategy was and explained that every rep would be accountable for executing it. By the end of the session, she'd given every rep a prospecting target and a plan to achieve it.

On my next check-in with this manager, she spilled over with enthusiasm as she described the team's progress. Since she'd taken charge of the prospecting strategy by empowering the team with prospecting goals, pipeline had grown significantly. Her people were inspired and ready to share their successes—and the big change, I knew, could be attributed to her ownership and reinforcement of the program. "We're getting better and better every day," she told me, and I knew that trend would continue for as long as she made it her job to lead and reinforce her reps' prospecting activities.

Getting started is the hardest. Once you show your commitment by your actions, your sales team will follow. Next, we dive into the tactics you can coach your teams to employ with their prospective buyers.

START WITH BUYER PRIORITIES

It does not matter what product or service you're selling or to whom; focusing on prospective buyer priorities should always be the first step in a successful prospecting strategy. Anchor your salespeople's prospecting strategies on buyer priorities.

Make a habit of sitting down with your salespeople to ask them what their buyer priorities are for the markets they cover. A short, simple list of concise buyer priorities is not as easy as one would think to create and share. Nevertheless, I encourage you to invest the time as a team to build a list of buyer profiles and their priorities. Use the tools and information created by marketing as a strong baseline of what buyers care most about. Then get really specific about what problems they need solved. The specificity is important, because these buyer priorities will become the foundation of every email, voicemail, and phone conversation your reps have with their prospects.

The chart on the next page is a visual representation of how to drive priorities through typical prospecting activity. Through the rest of the chapter, we'll examine some of its components.

Both sales managers and salespeople will benefit from a well-planned prospecting strategy that is grounded in what is most important to your buyers. A winning approach to prospecting starts with focusing on the buyer's priorities and tailoring every email, voicemail, and conversation to those priorities. It also involves your reps *not* just talking about their product or service. Showing a real understanding of the customer's main concerns makes a huge

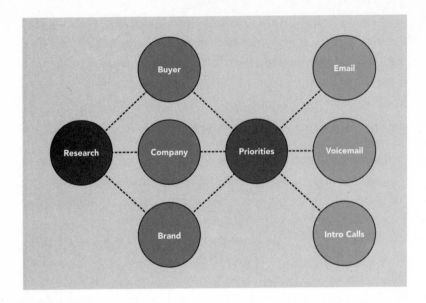

difference in prospecting effectiveness and lead conversion. I can speak pretty frankly about my experience as an executive at salesforce.com, during which time I received an abundance of emails every day. Some emails were automatically deleted. Some were filed away to maybe read later. And a select few I responded to fairly quickly. What set apart the ones I responded to right away? They were concise, personalized, and spoke to my priorities.

USE SOCIAL CHANNELS TO CONDUCT RESEARCH

Research is an important first step in uncovering buyer priorities, and fortunately, you and your reps have more research tools at your fingertips than ever. As you do your prospect research, look for trends and real-life stories that highlight priorities and challenges. When doing the research, have fun and bé curious. Note that the amount of research that is expected will vary depending on the qualification criteria needed to qualify your prospective buyers. For example, a business title may be used to prioritize leads in which C-level executives are classified as "tier 1," VPs and above are "tier 2," and managers and directors are "tier 3." The tier would dictate the amount of time spent doing the research before sending an email or calling. For example, a tier 3 lead might warrant five minutes of research, where a tier 1 might warrant thirty. It's good to set these best practices across your team and to be open to changing them as you learn more about your buyers and markets.

When a lead comes in, there are some ways you can use social channels to learn more about your prospect. We'll begin with LinkedIn, which is the industry-standard resource for finding buyers and career histories. It is easy to find out about executives and their teams. Go to LinkedIn, and before looking at someone's regular career history, find out whether you have any shared connections. It's always better to enrich a lead by making sure the first contact comes through a personal introduction from a mutual connection. Check the "People also viewed" section to get an idea of the person's team and peers; you can quickly begin to build an organizational picture using this LinkedIn feature.

Once you have profiled the buyer and understand what they do, whom they work for, and whom they know, you can turn your attention to their activity on other social media platforms. It's amazing how much people share in places like Twitter and Facebook—and how much you and your reps can learn from that sharing.

For the tier 1 leads (based on the criteria we identified earlier), I recommend finding the person's Twitter handle. Most CEOs and executives are active on Twitter these days, sharing a lot about what they are working on and what they are thinking. If you want to find out an executive's Twitter handle, simply Google the name and "Twitter." In addition to reading all their recent tweets to find out what's on their minds, you can also find out more about their networks and interests by looking at whom they are following—especially which accounts they started following most recently. This is something I always look at before I meet or talk to an executive.

I once received emails from a furniture company and an elevator company on the same day. The emails were very similar. Both companies had requested that I make an introduction to another executive at salesforce.com while this executive was in Japan. They wanted to talk about the new facilities opening in Japan and abroad. I was amazed at how these two companies had known exactly where this executive would be. There wasn't a public event scheduled, but it turns out that this executive had tweeted how excited he was to be going to Japan and in a subsequent tweet shared some detail on some new office locations planned for expansion. This story stuck with me because it represented a creativity that I admired and ultimately helped. I forwarded the notes mostly out of pure respect for the creativity used in this executive-prospecting outreach campaign.

Another benefit of doing social research is that it helps you and your reps understand the sentiment around a company and a brand; you can check out Twitter and official and unofficial Facebook groups to see what people are saying about the company. In addition, public job boards will share insights about where companies are hiring and the kinds of roles they are seeking to fill.

As you can see, there are abundant tools your team can use to conduct powerful social prospecting—and new tools are always being developed. The principles of social research apply to any social-media channel that exists today—and to those not created yet.

ENGAGE IN A PROSPECTING CONVERSATION

Once the research has been conducted, it's time for reps to begin a personalized conversation with the prospect. But getting responses to emails and voicemails is not easy. The salesperson's best chance is to inform her communications with the research she's done and to show that she understands the buyer's priorities.

I am a big fan of creating a conversation with a prospect. The right way to think about it is to create dialogue that is educational and provocative. I like to make sure that every time I reach out to a customer or prospect, I'm educating them about something. You should strive to have your prospects get value out of every interaction they have with your sales teams.

I get asked this question all the time: How many email and voicemail touches should we have with prospects? The answers will vary by company, industry, and sales segment. Use this section to help coach your sales teams and guide them as they do their own prospecting. I believe the right number lives somewhere between six and ten touches over a period that ranges from two to four weeks. Use this as a guideline, but nothing will replace asking your sales teams and looking at the data to make some firm best practice recommendations.

Look at creating a prospecting campaign that has six to ten touches and follows an email-voicemail pattern. First, send an email. Wait. Then make a phone call and leave a message if you don't get your executive on the phone. Don't stalk the prospects; give them some time to read their emails and listen to their voicemails. The emails need to be concise and to the point. Response rates improve dramatically when some basic prospecting guidelines are followed.

Write email copy that's focused on prospects' priorities. Personalize for top tiers. Be concise. Educate. Be provocative. Use a simple signature. There is no need to include your office phone, mobile phone, fax number, Twitter handle, and LinkedIn URL. Finally, avoid images, as they don't usually come through well on mobile devices and tend to send off an alert that the note is generated from a marketing template.

Encourage your team to keep emails simple. While it might seem easier to find that marketing template and do a mail merge, the reality is that nothing beats a personal note. I'm old-school this way; I'm a big believer in sending out handwritten thank-you notes. People appreciate the effort, especially when the note has clearly been personalized.

Every part of the email structure is space that can be used to educate and engage in a conversation. Coach your teams to use the subject-line real estate wisely to highlight a key business issue. Executives make a lot of decisions in that split second they have when they scan the subject lines in their inboxes. Be friendly in the opening, using words like "hi" and "hello." Be human. Jump right in and answer the question of why the customer should care. Share a provocative or challenging statistic that becomes the heart of the email. It's the "so what." A good salesperson will identify an issue or priority, then map a statistic that implies a pain or gain that the recipient can quickly quantify. These behaviors drive action and replies. Leave them with something to read or watch that supports the argument being made in the email. And end with the meeting or conversation request. No business title at the end; just a simple name and phone number. Remember, the more times you remind your sales teams to not sell in email but to engage in a conversation, the better the team performance will be.

Use this email template and "rinse and repeat" across the prospecting campaign. Change the messages a bit. Share new statistics and thought-provoking questions. Leave additional videos to watch and documents to read. The connection is the core business issue that is most important to the executive buyer.

Another great approach is to empower sales teams to collaborate and create great email templates together. Have them share the emails that they are proud of and that worked. Combine the best of the best. Challenge the team to come up with great emails that will elicit great replies and will become the best practices used by other sales teams.

I was working with a team that decided to create their email templates based on the ones provided by marketing. It was empowering

Email Example

I'd like to share some fascinating sales performance statistics from a global study conducted by YOUR COMPANY that is very eye opening to executives like you.

- Provocative statistic #1
- Provocative statistic #2
- Provocative statistic #3

YOUR PRODUCT is helping companies improve these statistics. You can watch this customer video to hear their stories.When is a good time to schedule 15 minutes to have an introductory conversation about your business challenges?

YOUR NAME
YOUR PHONE NUMBER

and helped them own the messages. It's a great best practice that I recommend every sales manager adopt with his or her teams.

Leaving voicemails is a big part of a successful prospecting strategy, too. Keep voice messages short and punchy. You lose the listener after the first twenty to thirty seconds. Do not sell your product on the voice message; instead, focus on a top executive priority. Make it all about them and their challenges. Focus on one point to make. Be friendly. Smile. End with their name. It's a nice, personal touch, and it improves the response rates.

• • •

I've shared a lot of prospecting tips and best practices in this chapter, primarily because prospecting is not easy. Some salespeople do love it, but plenty of others hate it. There is tension between sales and marketing about lead quality and quantity not meeting expectations. Getting an entire team focused on a common set of prospecting goals, using a set of tools that are compelling to buyers, and exceeding pipeline goals will take time. It won't be solved in one training session or one sales meeting. I'm a firm believer in iterating sales programs and making tweaks to email templates and voicemails in real time with a team rather than trying to create the perfect program from day one. Be flexible and empower your teams to experiment, as long as they come back and share what worked and what didn't work.

CHAPTER 11

BE CURIOUS

In the previous chapter, I said that when I meet with sales managers for the first time, I always ask whether their main problem is creating more pipeline or accelerating their deals in the pipeline. If it's the former, we work on beefing up prospecting strategy. But if it's the latter—if deals lack urgency and are getting stalled out before the close—we go straight into talking about another tenet of the sales manager's duties: ensuring that reps are actively curious throughout the selling process.

Curiosity is a driving force of the sales process. When all your team members are actively cultivating their own interest in their customers—when they're asking the right questions and taking the time to listen to an executive's problems, understand their business, and find ways to help them—they'll build long-lasting relationships. Being curious about your customer's business problems helps uncover why they are buying, resulting in better qualification and forecasting accuracy. Use discovery best practices and old-fashioned curiosity to uncover why customers need to buy and why they need to buy *now*.

Some salespeople are natural pros in this area, while others may struggle. For many reps, it's tempting to focus on what the product or service has to offer to the prospect. It's your job as sales manager to constantly remind people of the power of asking questions and staying curious, giving them a framework for continuing to discover the prospect's priorities once the customer is in the pipeline.

I've witnessed many sales teams coming together right before a meeting with a very important executive, and typically they have spent a ton of time crafting messaging, building a presentation, and preparing demonstrations based on their presumed knowledge of the executive's priorities. Preparation is a good thing, but if the rep goes into the meeting and bludgeons the executive with information, the sale is probably not going to go forward.

A good sales manager will ask, "What's our agenda for this meeting?" When the sales team replies, "Here's our agenda, presentation, and custom demonstration!" the manager will reply, "No! In this meeting we're going to listen, and then listen more. And what will we do when we're finished listening? We'll listen more."

That's the power of listening and curiosity. As Epictetus, a Greek philosopher, said, "We have two ears and one mouth so that we can listen twice as much as we speak." The simplicity and magic of simply listening is a true game changer in the world of sales.

Barry Rhein, a pioneer and visionary in sales training, first developed the phrase *Selling Through Curiosity*™.[23] When I was at salesforce.com, we partnered with Barry on a number of key initiatives focused on making salespeople more curious in the spirit of helping customers solve their most important business problems.

In my early conversations with Barry, he gave me a potent summary of the benefits of curiosity in sales:

1. What if there was a way for your salespeople to understand your customers better than anyone else, and to gain a clear and powerful advantage over your competition?

2. What if you could create so much value in your customers' mind that they would want your solution, no matter what the price?

3. What if you could set yourself apart from the competition quickly and win all the business?

Being curious is about becoming a master at information gathering. It's about seeing yourself as a business anthropologist.[24] It's about cultivating that wide-eyed, insatiable, childlike hunger for more information. Many salespeople let these important skills atrophy in their day-to-day interactions with customers and prospects. Fortunately, you can give them a framework for listening and questioning that will forever transform the way your sales teams do discovery.

By injecting questioning and discovery into the sales process, your sales teams will

- qualify prospects faster and more effectively;
- better understand prospect's business challenges;
- better understand the prospect's decision-making process; and
- develop better solutions to meet the prospect's needs.

And what does that mean for you, the sales manager? Well, it means that your team will be better equipped to meet its numbers, that your forecast accuracy will improve, and that you'll have a lot fewer sluggish, faltering deals clogging up the pipeline. Being curious and thoughtful about discovery will result in many fewer "no-decision" deals, too.

CURIOSITY IN CUSTOMER MEETINGS

There are a number of best practices that should be employed before you walk in to meet any customer or executive for the first time. Share them with your sales teams on a regular basis. It helps to be prepared, and these rules will better prepare you and your sales teams. Here's a condensed list:

- Treat every customer meeting as a discovery meeting.
- Do your homework on customer challenges and executive priorities.
- Use social media, public information, and pre-meeting interviews to augment your meeting preparation.
- Start every meeting with the customer sharing his or her top priorities and goals.
- Always ask open-ended questions.
- Ask layering questions to really understand priorities and challenges. Be curious.
- Resist the urge to pitch your product (in early-stage meetings).
- Be open to the conversation going in a different direction than expected.
- If you are confused, it means you are learning more about your customer.
- Learning something new is like finding gold. Celebrate it.
- Listen more than you talk.
- Close every meeting with a summary of what you heard and a clear set of actions.

After salespeople listen to executive top priorities and relay back verbally in the meeting what they heard, they frequently miss an important step. All too often, they do not take the time to document what they heard and share it back with the executive, using their own words. The medium employed in this sharing is irrelevant—the salesperson can do it in an email, a follow-up phone call, or a pre-pared document. The point is to demonstrate that you understand the buyer's priorities and to get any feedback on parts you may have wrong. This is important, because one of the biggest complaints companies have when they work with sales teams is that the sales reps did not listen to their needs.

Doing this sets a salesperson on the path toward creating a customized, value-based solution that meets a company's needs, every time. The formula is based on using the words, stories, and examples shared in presentations, demonstrations, and proposals—over and over. Over the years, I have called this type of customer-engagement exercise "creating a shared vision."[25] Using phrases like *shared vision* helps align customer needs with expectations and ultimately with a value-based solution. Such phrases also enable a sales team to be transparent with a customer about how the selling process meets the buying process. You also know that your customer is engaged when they redline the shared vision document and send it back to you. When the customers send a shared vision document back with edits, you know they are interested in solving their problem together.

Once the salespeople share with an executive in a written form what they heard during the interview, they immediately engage a buying process that is differentiated and unique to them. But most salespeople do not engage in this fashion. This is why it is neces-sary to also remind your sales teams that the customer is always right and that maybe what your sales team heard was not exactly what the executive said. It is okay to collect feedback and update the list of priorities based on that feedback. The iteration of messaging and the surfacing of problems with an executive will make presentations interactive and will increase the likelihood of success in winning the deal.

Remember, this chapter is about listening and curiosity, and this is the best way to showcase listening skills. Listen first and, chances are, your customers will believe you will listen later if things do not go as smoothly as you or they like. Problems occur—it happens—and establishing an open relationship based on trust, listening, and collaboration is the only way to win over executives. Always get accurate feedback from your customer each step of the way and know where you stand in terms of winning their business.

The benefits of exhibiting curiosity to prospects are huge. Your sales teams will be able to more effectively link customized value to pricing in a way that allows your customer to justify paying more. You will differentiate yourselves relative to your competition. You will lead and control your sales process.

I have a friend who closed one of the largest transactions in the history of the company where he works—less than twelve months after he started. It was a truly life-changing event for him and for everyone that witnessed the recognition (and check) he received. He was recognized as a top performer and was handed a "big-ass" check on stage for the huge deal closed. There was a standing ovation in the room at the sales kickoff event. Everyone stood there in awe, anxiously waiting to hear his story.

I asked him: "How did you do it? What was your secret? What products and services did you sell?" His answer: "I solved the customer's biggest problem."

It's a remarkable story with lessons that are universal for every salesperson. During his account research and due diligence, he learned everything he could about the company, their industry, and their customers' buying experience. He took what he observed, learned, and concluded and went right up to the top of the executive chain to have a thoughtful executive-discovery conversation with the CEO of the company. He uncovered the company's and the CEO's top business problem. He used that information in every subsequent interaction with every stakeholder in the buying process. He focused his energy and sales activity to solve the company's most critical business issue. That's how he was able to close the biggest deal in his company's history.

This salesperson went in to a prospect account and related with the CEO at a business-issue and emotional level. He avoided positioning and selling products and services. Instead, this salesperson was maniacally focused on getting his entire sales team, including all headquarters staff, aligned with the need to solve this critical business issue that he discovered for one reason only: because he was curious.

THE DISCOVERY MAP

I have always found it useful to build a framework to help visualize concepts. Here is a discovery framework you can share with your team that they can start using immediately. You can customize it to your business, too, so it becomes part of your culture. It is important to use words and phrases that map to your sales culture, just like your sales values. The framework should also correlate with your sales process. The goal of the framework is to create a set of consistent sales actions (and questions) that will help uncover compelling events and drive urgency.

The discovery framework includes the topics and a "questioning tree" that can be used to remind salespeople about the sequence of how to be curious, listen, listen more, ask the right questions, and then come back with a high-value solution.

Discovery Drives Trust

Today

Issues

Compelling Event

Tomorrow

Outcomes

Criteria

Today

Start by understanding how a company is structured today. Get to the heart of what's working and ultimately what's not working for the business. Find out what they do, whom they sell to, and what they sell. Most if not all of this should be uncovered through thoughtful discovery. You want your sales team to use this information to inform a high-quality discovery conversation.

Issues

Focus on the most important business challenges. Depending on whom you are meeting with, focus on corporate challenges, business unit challenges, or even a department's challenges. It is important to get a clear picture of what is happening inside the company and what macroeconomic trends in their industry are top-of-mind. Once you have a clear view of the top challenges, dive into each one and uncover the top priorities or initiatives. This is where you want to better understand how these priorities impact an executive's personal priorities and goals.

Compelling Events

From issues, you want to begin to unravel top business initiatives to get to a compelling event. Uncover compelling events through thoughtful discovery and a good understanding of what the business initiatives are and when they need to be solved.

Tomorrow

Now that you have the context of the challenges and a clear set of priorities, you are ready to start creating a compelling story based on real people, products, and experiences (more on telling stories in chapter 12). The more detailed you can get in the documentation of the "as-is" and "to-be" user stories, the greater the likelihood you will be able to create a compelling value proposition. Use real names and real job titles.

Outcomes

It is very important to map out the key benefits that improvements to the issues will have. The benefits should be personal, should impact the people, and should also relate back to the top priorities and key challenges; it should all tie together. The benefits should be financial, yielding real value in terms of revenue gains, cost reduction, improvements in productivity, or other tangible business benefits. Include both quantifiable and nonquantifiable benefits. It always helps to develop a set of success metrics that are determined from the outset of a project.

Criteria

All salespeople should be reminded to be just as curious about the decision-making process and evaluation criteria as they are about a company's business issues and challenges. Solving business issues that are tied to a compelling event usually involves a formal decision-making process and evaluation criteria that need to be fully understood.

ASKING THE RIGHT QUESTIONS

Reminding your sales team to always focus on getting answers to the top qualification questions will remind them of the need to do discovery the right way. Asking great questions is a very important sales skill every salesperson should have. When your reps are asking open-ended, layered questions, they will better qualify opportunities and accounts.

Zig Ziglar wrote that "every sale has five basic obstacles: no need, no money, no hurry, no desire, no trust." Here is a set of questions that should be a part of every salesperson's repertoire to help overcome these five basic obstacles. These questions should not replace the power of open-ended questions but should anchor opportunity qualification. If a salesperson internalizes these questions in his sales activity, he will improve his sales skills and drive better forecast accuracy.

What are they buying? Get crystal clarity on what solutions your customers are interested in buying. What they are buying should map back to their challenges and have a clear sense of need and priority.

Why are they buying? *Why* a customer is buying should be tied to a specific event and top company priority. Focus on the corporate needs along with the personal needs of the buyers.

When are they buying? Identify and focus on compelling events. Tie a decision to a specific date that is meaningful to your customers, such as their fiscal year, a board decision, or even some kind of company kickoff event. Compelling events are not created; they are uncovered.

Who is buying? Identifying buyers and influencers is key to mapping out the steps to close and the actions required to win over every executive. Consider all the influencers, even the ones that are not so obvious. Invest the time early to build a proper organization influence and political map to avoid surprises late in the sales cycle.

Who is paying? A common question that is not usually answered until too late in every sales cycle sheds light on the decision-making process within a prospect. Find out who is paying and understand the customer's decision-making process. Sometimes even though an executive champion makes a decision, procurement or finance approval can take weeks or months.

These are great, foundational questions, but if they want to get the benefit out of asking them, your reps will have to listen closely to what the prospect says in response—and, just as important, what the prospect *doesn't* say. Many salespeople have "happy ears"; they want to believe they are ready to close a deal. Every salesperson wants to think he or she is talking with the right buyer and that the buyer has power and can drive consensus. Successful salespeople recognize the happy ears syndrome, however, and learn to ask "why not" questions rather than "why yes" questions.

I was once spending time with a customer, and the buyer was telling me everything I wanted to hear. The deal would get done by the end of the month. . . . The budget was approved. . . . The PO would get signed. I didn't ask if there was any reason why this deal would not get signed. But the deal didn't get signed, and I learned an important lesson about how to avoid happy ears. The best salespeople focus on what they do not know and work hard to get those answers.

Focusing on critical business issues will empower salespeople to become more strategic, to really know buyer priorities, and to identify top initiatives. For example, some top buyer priorities for a CMO include measuring a marketing program's ROI, building pipeline, and driving branding consistency across all properties. On the other hand, a head of sales might be interested in revenue growth, improving forecast accuracy, and driving up productivity. With buyer priorities in mind, solve issues that drive financial impact. Look for problems that increase revenues, reduce costs, and/or improve customer acquisition.

Uncovering critical business issues will lead your salespeople to a company's top initiatives and then to a compelling event, which is the salesperson's Holy Grail. I'm reminded of an approach someone shared with me called "top five initiatives."

The "top five" approach consists of making sure that the problems you are solving for a prospect are correlated to a company's top five business initiatives. As an executive, there are only so many initiatives and priorities one can handle at any given time. It's your job as a sales manager to help your sales reps be critical about how well the solution they are recommending fits into a company's top five priorities. Encourage your salespeople to employ this technique regularly to ensure that they're truly addressing the needs of the prospect and helping move the deal through the pipeline.

USING CURIOSITY TO UNCOVER COMPELLING EVENTS

There is no sales team in the world that will not benefit from a focused and interactive discussion around what is and what is not a compelling event. As you know from chapter 4, this is the world-recognized definition of what a compelling event is and is not:

A compelling event is a *time-sensitive* response to an *internal* or *external* business pressure that drives *action* within a defined time period with *consequences of inactions*.

Every time I talk to a sales team about compelling events, a debate happens. Can compelling events be created? Are they only uncovered? Or, are they a result of great discovery that identifies business issues that are tied back to a compelling event?

The debate is a good one to have for many reasons. I was facilitating a compelling-events discussion with a sales team. The team pushed me on the idea that they could create compelling events. I asked them to share what some of the compelling events were, and they shared events like a price promotion, a month-end discount, a year-end discount, and their CEO being available for an executive visit.

I had heard of sales teams using the promotional discounts as a catalyst to drive a deal, but I had not heard someone equate an executive visit with a compelling event. Why would the fact that a company's CEO visited a customer result in a salesperson thinking they had a compelling event? I decided to use this example as a discussion point with the team.

The discussion turned into a heated debate. In the end, the room came to the conclusion that an executive visit, while important to the buying process, is not a compelling event. A CEO visit to a customer is not an internal or external business issue resulting in an action that would result in a consequence if it did not happen.

After the meeting, the sales manager expressed appreciation for the conversation and the debate. He believed that the sales team's skills had been developed in this area. Sometimes it takes a discussion and debate to help a sales team learn from each other.

Remember that salespeople learn best from each other. It's the job of the sales manager to understand where the team is and to facilitate a conversation that respects everyone's experiences and ideas of what a compelling event is.

I formally experienced compelling events in my early days of selling, specifically when we created the Partner Relationship Management category in the late 1990s. We had developed an amazing enterprise software solution that was not selling as fast as we would have liked. We decided we had to drive urgency. I know the theory says you cannot create a compelling event, but what we learned is that you can map executive priorities to an event that is already scheduled or to an event that drives business goals. The challenge then is to get your project prioritized higher up on the list of competing corporate priorities. With this Partner Relationship Management solution, we connected our solution with an upcoming partner conference to drive urgency and a faster buy decision. The partner conference was happening. Our job was to map the value of our solution to the goals of the event.

A compelling event for a marketing executive like a chief marketing officer could be a product launch or a campaign that needs to happen by a certain date. Having to get a new website up by a certain date is another great one. If selling to a head of sales, tie your solution and value to events like sales kickoffs or new-hire start dates. For IT, their need to retire old infrastructure or application technology by a certain date can provide you with a compelling event.

Remember that for any of these to be a compelling event, it must have a specific date attached to it and a consequence of no action.

I encourage you to have a compelling event sales huddle regularly, as part of your training program, either in person or virtually. It will help sales teams:

1. align on what is and is not a compelling event;

2. avoid conversations with empty promises;

3. create urgency over competing priorities;

4. build a list of compelling events; and

5. avoid "happy ears."

Here is a sales huddle best practice that I have run with several companies. Most want to do this every month, as the deals are always changing and you can never have enough of uncovering compelling events. Have your reps go through these two exercises. They will help drive urgency in accounts and in sales campaigns against their deals.

The compelling event definition and subsequent questions will form the foundation for all learning, discovery, and qualification of deals by the sales team.

Personal Story Exercise: Have each person on the team share a "Happy Ears" example.

Every team member shares an example of an executive assertion that was too good to be true. Inspire each salesperson to pick a deal or a buyer and share the happy ears experience with the team. They also share what they would do differently today.

Deal Review Exercise: Have each person share an active deal and the compelling event, along with a specific date.

Every team member shares an example of a compelling event in an active deal. The power of applying the theory to the real deal is huge. Every salesperson selects one deal and shares the compelling event, including the date, the business pressure, and the consequence of no decision. The team votes on whether they agree or not. Every time one of these sales huddles happens, the collective learning that happens is amazing for productivity. Execution changes immediately, as the deal realizations can be applied right away to more deals in the pipeline.

- What is the compelling event?
- What is the compelling event date?
- What problem are you solving?
- What is the value to the buyer?
- What happens if they do nothing?

UNDERSTANDING THE PROSPECT'S DECISION-MAKING PROCESS

Finding out about your prospect's business and priorities is vital, but so is understanding how the purchase decision will ultimately be made. If your team isn't asking questions to understand who has the final say on the deal, they're not going to be as effective as they could be.

When I was very young, working in my father's retail furniture store in Toronto, I learned the concept of the decision-making process. I didn't have a formal name for this important sales process skill when I was young. However, we did know that the likelihood that a customer would buy a piece of furniture was much higher if we could diagnose who was the buyer and who was the influencer in the decision to buy a sofa or dining room set. There were a few cues that my father coached me on to help us determine how to relate with every customer.

A family would walk into my dad's furniture store on a lovely summer day in Toronto. I would greet them at the door and offer my assistance. Imagine a typical family of four. The parents of this family would quickly start looking around while the kids were asked to sit down and behave. We strategically sat them next to a fun piece of furniture that could act like a jungle gym. We kept them happy and occupied. The family was looking for a new dining room set.

Within the first couple of minutes, based on eye gestures back and forth between the parents, I could tell what the game plan was going to be. When I asked, "How could I help you?" I watched who answered and who stepped forward. The parent who would make the decision on style, color, and comfort would already be sitting down on a chair, touching the wood table, and feeling the softness of the fabric. The other parent would step back and wait. In some cases, the identification of who made the product choice would be even more direct, with a hand gesture or even a statement about that person being the boss.

Because I had been trained by my dad to identify these cues, I knew exactly what my focus was for the next five to ten minutes. I was there to answer every technical question for the evaluator and key influencer in this decision. We were in the zone to meet the buyer's evaluation criteria. I would start asking questions to uncover relative importance of evaluation criteria like price, value, and comfort. They would have questions about how to care for and clean the product. Comfort was also part of the evaluation criteria. I made sure I asked one of the most important decision-making process and evaluation questions: How do you feel about this piece of furniture?

At some point after meeting the influencer's evaluation criteria, an ideal dining room would be identified and selected. The energy would shift from the first parent to the second parent as the conversation shifted from product to money.

The parent who was looking at all the dining room styles

would send another cue, either an eye gesture or maybe even a bold statement to the effect of, "I like this one." The other parent would then step in and begin asking questions about price, payment terms, and delivery options. We were in closing mode; they were ready to buy. We had successfully met the needs of the first parent while keeping the children occupied. Terms would be discussed and payment made.

There are many lessons in this retail-selling story that apply to sales cycles in many industries. The decision-making process is a universal concept. The complexity of a decision-making process varies dramatically depending on the scope and size of the problem being solved. The main point is that every salesperson needs to be aware of what the decision-making process and evaluation criteria are for their buyers from day one. The goal is to avoid late-deal surprises.

The retail-furniture sales example demonstrates the importance of understanding a customer's decision-making process and evaluation criteria. Top sales executives all over the world embrace these foundational skills. During my career at salesforce.com, the salespeople we brought up on stage at sales kickoffs to recognize as top performers and the ones that earned the largest commission checks knew this, too.

As a sales manager, you'll want to make sure that understanding a customer's decision-making process is part of the cadence of how your team runs their business. You'll want to make sure they have a strategy for uncovering this information early and often in every sales cycle. You'll want to coach your teams to "follow the money." What I mean by this is you want to make sure that you have accounted for every last detail, down to whose finger will hit the "approve" button on a purchase order you are hoping to to get signed. The last thing you want to learn is that someone is on vacation and you can't get your deal done because the sales team didn't have the detail on the decision-making process.

Every company's decision-making process is unique. The job of the sales team is to be "just as curious about the decision-making process as they are about the customer's business problems." Barry Rhein showed me how important it is to apply the principles of discovery to a customer's decision-making process. Some companies, depending on the size of a transaction, may allow decisions to be made at the line-manager or departmental levels. Others will need to go up to a CFO, CEO, or even the board for approval. It's important to have clarity on who is buying, who is paying, and how a decision will be made. And don't forget to ask the critical question of whether anyone has veto power. I also love this open-ended question: Who else needs to be part of the process?

The same energy and curiosity should be applied to the evaluation criteria. You want to find out what is important to the decision makers and influencers and, more importantly, why it is important. Some companies may value price over product superiority; you can easily turn pricing objections into a strategic differentiator if you understand what is motivating an evaluation criterion. Also, asking layered questions around the evaluation criteria will surface stakeholders who were not already identified.

A great coaching tip for your sales teams is one around handling objections. If a buyer believes you cannot meet one of the items on a list of evaluation criteria, there is a suggested way to handle it, and there is no need to be defensive with a response. Simply reply with a question: What would you need to see to believe we can meet your requirements?

* * *

A tweet from Simon Sinek effectively sums up the message you want to send your salespeople: "Listening is not understanding the words of the questions asked; listening is understanding why the question was asked in the first place."

The most successful salespeople are those who have great listening skills, and when you drive a culture of listening, curiosity, questioning, and discovery, everyone wins: you, your reps, your company—and your customers.

CHAPTER 12

TELL GREAT STORIES

Storytelling is a great way to establish credibility with customers and prospects. Every salesperson aims to tell great customer stories, and my experience tells me that the best storytellers are the best salespeople—and vice versa. A great customer storyteller can understand customers and relate to them in a compelling way, capturing their imaginations and taking them to a place that will solve all of their problems. Storytelling should be a central part of your sales team's DNA, culture, and sales values. Every rep on your team should be telling stories rather than pitching products; this approach drives trust and—perhaps counterintuitively—urgency as well. As the authors of *What Great Sales People Do* write, "Nothing moves people more than authentic storytelling."[26] Stories help salespeople overcome objections, build confidence, and propel action. Compelling stories can also empower compelling events.

A great storyteller knows the story, understands it, internalizes it, and is able to retell it in his own words. He knows how to make it emotional and memorable. He avoids pitching the features of his products and services, focusing instead on real business problems and business value. In this chapter, I will share examples that highlight why storytelling is an important part of the sales process and should be a skill that every salesperson on your team masters. There is a formula to telling a good story, and as with every other selling skill we've talked about so far, it's your responsibility to inspire your team to employ it effectively and consistently.

ONCE UPON A TIME . . .

A few years back, my team and I had a meeting with the president of one of the largest hard-drive companies in the world. It would be our first meeting with this executive, and the goal of the meeting was to share some best practices and examples of how other high-technology companies like his were using our service. We were employing a sales value that we called "Users sell for you"—implying that sharing customer stories is an effective way to build confidence and credibility to close deals. The meeting was scheduled and we strategized as a team to prepare. We had presentations, demonstrations, and a host of materials ready. We were ready for any request. When we met on-site with the customer, the top executive asked a very direct question of me: "Tell me a story of how a company like mine is using your service and realizing value."

I was ready with a customer story that matched this company's profile, including business challenges, size of company, and industry. "Let me tell you a story of a very similar company to yours," I began. My story lasted for ten minutes, and I didn't use any slides or demonstrations. It was about how the Dell Corporation uses salesforce.com to improve their business, driving up sales productivity, partner revenues, and customer intimacy. The story we told was shared from the view of the CEO, Michael Dell, creating a clear visual for the customer to visualize the future. We created a

peer-to-peer relationship between the executive in the room wanting to hear a customer story and the executive we were referencing.
We successfully created urgency and elicited feelings of emotion
supported by quantifiable value.

I told it as it had actually happened and shared real examples of
benefit and value from the perspective of the company's employees,
partners, and customers. I shared how the company improved its
revenues, customer satisfaction, and shareholder value.

At the end of the story, the president of this company uttered
these three words to his team: "I want that."

Your goal is to make every one of your customers say that about
your products and services.

Storytelling should be part of every salesperson's talk track and
sales tools. Marketing should always include stories in the corporate
and product presentations. Stories should be printed and in video.
Salespeople should appreciate that they can differentiate themselves
by telling compelling stories rather than by pitching products. Telling a story that ignites a CEO's imagination or compels a president
to demand that action be taken immediately is a desired outcome
of a great conversation grounded in customer storytelling. My goal
is to help every salesperson be a better storyteller and to help sales
managers remind and coach their sales teams to make this a priority
in every sales campaign.

Customer storytelling should come from the heart; it should
be emotional, personalized, and quantifiable. Part of your job as
a sales manager is to assess your team and empower them to self-
assess. Do they tell stories that touch the human spirit? Are the
stories emotional? Do your stories highlight financial benefits that
are quantifiable? Have your sales teams rate themselves on their
storytelling abilities and then share with each other their relative
strengths and weaknesses. Have storytelling be a part of coaching,
one-on-ones, and performance reviews. Celebrate great storytellers and share their best practices across your team.

THE ANATOMY OF A GREAT STORY

We can all be better customer storytellers. Use the principles of customer storytelling to transform a narrative anchored in a PowerPoint slide into something that is really compelling and motivates action. Your goal is to bring your prospective buyer into the story and make her feel as if she is a part of that story.

There are many companies today that have a secret sauce for telling a great story and coaching salespeople to tell great stories. The purpose here is to give you a simple framework that you can apply immediately in your coaching conversations and ultimately sales campaigns, too. If you and your teams can really master storytelling, you will connect with your customer and prospects like never before. Telling an impactful customer story starts by identifying the right company that maps to the industry, size of company, and business challenges, so that the story rings true. Be thoughtful about correlating customer stories and references to prospective buyers.

Here are some simple steps you can use to inspire customers with great, compelling stories:

- **Set the context.** It all starts here. Share what is going on in the industry and with the company. Talk about the competition. Dive into what challenges this company was trying to solve. Focus on the critical business issues. Be concise and use a minute or two to cover this important stage.

- **Show them their future.** Start the story with a promise of the outcome. Show your prospects their future. Give them a glimpse into what their world will look after they go through the same transformation as the customer in the story. Give them the business benefits and the punch line right at the beginning, after you have set the context.

- **Put yourself in their shoes.** Know your audience. Identify characters. Make the story personal by role. Use relevant examples. Talk at the right level.

- **Know their pains.** Go back in time and tell the story of pain. Identify the villains. What challenges existed for this company and this executive? Demonstrate that you understand their problems around competition, market share, revenue, and culture. You've already shared the context; this is where you can share some of the back story and the detail that maps to the person's profile.

- **Share the steps in their journey.** Walk your customer through the journey, starting with the first meeting and sharing key milestones. Be as detailed and thorough as possible. This is where you will win them over and make them feel that you have the capacity to make them successful. Focus on your experience and how the customer will benefit by having you along on this journey with other companies just like them.

- **Close with a reference offer.** Offer customer reference details. Broker the introduction. Brief your prospect and customer. Send thank-you notes.

COACH AND PRACTICE STORYTELLING

In the spirit of salespeople learning from salespeople, here is a storytelling sales huddle that is easy to run, in person or virtually, and has very high impact. Telling stories is fun, so why not make learning and practicing fun, too? Why not even push the envelope and make it competitive? Use the principles of sales huddles we introduced earlier in the book; encourage salespeople to learn from each other. Add competition and crowdsourcing, and run your own customer storytelling sales huddle. Salespeople love the program, and it can be run over and over. There is no shortage of the need for salespeople to learn more customer stories.

Have every person on your team select a customer story that they want to share with their colleagues. They can tell the story in a sales huddle, or you can have them record the customer story and share it with everyone in a video. Keep the feedback positive and constructive. It is okay for the team to realize that they're not the best storytellers. By putting themselves out there and practicing customer storytelling in a group setting, your salespeople will improve their skills. A bit of vulnerability will go a long way with this skill because the more one steps up and presents, the more feedback one will get. This is why they're doing this exercise—to get better. Here again is a benefit of the SalesHood community concept: By learning from and with each other, your sales team is being transformed, member by member, into even more productive salespeople.

There are so many benefits to running this kind of exercise on a quarterly basis with your teams. You build the storytelling muscle inside your sales organization. Each person will put his or her best foot forward to tell the most compelling and engaging story. You can create a competition where the team votes on the best story. What is also happening is that you're building your library of customer stories through crowdsourcing. You build a bigger database of customer stories for your sales teams to share with their customers and prospects. You have salespeople learning best practices in storytelling from salespeople. You're stressing the importance of customer storytelling. And by the way, these stories that usually remain tucked away in the minds of your sales teams are now getting documented and even video-recorded. I love this exercise because it truly accomplishes so many goals at once.

As much as you can, drive storytelling in everything you do. Have your salespeople begin conversations and demonstrations with customer stories. Have them open up meetings with customer stories. Their consistent use of the phrase "Let me tell you a story" will immediately build trust with customers.

CUSTOMER STORYTELLING AND PITCH BEST PRACTICES

I hosted a meeting with a group of sales managers to share best practices around customer presentations and "pitch" presentations. Even though some might frown upon the word *pitch*, for its negative presentation sentiment, the concept is still strong. We agreed that the criteria of what makes a great pitch has evolved from selling to solving problems, from a monologue to a dialogue, and from talking to a prospect to engaging in a collaborative conversation.

I believe the word *pitch* still works and the group of sales managers and I talked about resetting their sales teams on the attributes of a winning pitch and great customer engagements. Here is the output of a list of pitch best practices created by a group of sales managers. This is a great example of crowdsourcing sales best practices from sales leaders.

1. **Listen and let the customer talk first**. Start the meeting by asking a few simple questions: "I'm prepared to discuss our solution for you, but has anything changed since we last spoke?" or "Is there anything else I need to know before diving into the presentation?" Remind your sales team of the importance of keeping your customers talking.

2. **Have an agenda**. It's a simple idea but so critical. It sets the tone and improves the professionalism of the experience. We all know we need to do it. The sales managers in the discussion aligned on making it mandatory in every customer meeting and even internal meetings, too.

3. **Focus on customer business problems**. Rather than be product focused, have the context of the meeting always be about the customer. Solve big problems and keep the meeting (and sales teams) focused on the value of solving those problems.

4. **Ask questions**. Always be curious and ask open-ended questions. Pause in meetings to check in with customers to see if they're getting what they expected from their time investment.

5. **Make it conversational**. The meeting isn't a keynote address and should not be a monologue. Many times sales managers end up stepping in to help a meeting that is a bit dry and boring by engaging customers in a conversation. This always becomes a great coaching opportunity.

6. **Respect time constraints**. Be professional and mindful about the meeting time. Note that there are time constraints on both sides. Set the right expectation from the beginning and check in on progress.

7. **Customize to your customer**. The top sales managers appreciate marketing presentations, especially ones that can be easily customized to meet customer needs. Use your customer's logos, language, and stories to paint a picture of their future.

8. **Share next steps**. An important part of every meeting is moving the deal forward. A great way to do it is to be transparent about next steps. Just like an agenda, make a next-steps slide or conversation a part of every meeting format.

9. **Practice the pitch**. I was reminded of the importance of this part of the pitch. It's important to practice the pitch with

the sales team but even more important to practice the pitch with your customer champion or internal coach, too.

10. **Turn your pitch into a story**. One sales manager shared that she has her salespeople do the pitch without the slides in a dry run or a practice session to make it more of a story. Start with why the meeting is happening and the expected outcomes. Outline the customer challenges and pain. Map the problems to business value and quantify it as best as you can. Share customer proof points. Explain how this solution can become reality. Then close with next steps.

CREATE A LIBRARY OF CUSTOMER STORIES AND SALES REFERENCES

One of the most important currencies a salesperson has is customer stories. They want stories that they can use to meet customer objections and exceed customer dreams. The best sales managers I have worked with took customer stories and sales references very seriously. It became part of the team's culture and DNA. The best of the best took control and maintained lists of their best references and customer stories for the team. The technology question of how to store these references is the easy part of this equation; the hard part is the discipline to create and maintain a library of customer stories that are industry specific and local.

Important note: These relationships need to be nurtured and not overused. Customer reference fatigue is common, and building a larger list is a great way to spread the reference calls across a wider net of customer accounts. To build a ready library of diverse customer stories, crowdsource your sales teams to share stories either in written form or, even better, in video format.

BUILD YOUR SALES REFERENCES PROGRAMS

Having your sales reps tell stories to prospects is fantastic, but there's something even better: having your *customers* tell stories to prospects. The salesforce.com model is a great one to follow; a quick look at their YouTube channel or keynote addresses highlights the power of storytelling and reference selling. Integrating customer stories early and often in the sales process is a principle that any company of any size should adopt. Larger companies have the luxury of staffing up a full sales references program, but smaller companies need to coach salespeople to own the entire life-cycle of a sales reference.

A well-oiled sales references program is a bit like a matchmaking service. You are matching companies that are successfully using your product or service with companies that want to achieve similar successes. Consider matching companies based on the following attributes:

- company size
- industry
- geography
- business problem
- solution

When an interested prospect is ready to engage in a reference conversation, there are some best practices that should be employed to increase the likelihood of a great outcome. Make sure you brief both parties, either by phone or at least with an email note. Broker the introduction and then let these two executives have a private conversation. How you brief your reference and your prospective buyer is so critical; give your sales reference the insights they need to know about the sales campaign and your buyer. Give them as much context as possible since they are now part of the extended sales team. You want to make sure they reinforce your sales strategy and value. Share the questions you expect to come up on the call and prepare for the best answers. With your prospective buyer, make sure the reference has all the details of the products and services they are using and their history with your company. Let them know what to expect from the call and also what not to expect from the call.

• • •

When I think of the power of stories in the selling process, I'm reminded of my children and how much fun we have reading books and telling each other stories. Think of the glimmer in a child's eye when you ask her if she wants to read a story. Who doesn't want to hear a story? Customer storytelling will let guards down and get prospects relaxed. Stories that are emotional, quantifiable, and personalized will drive urgency and action. Above all, remember that a great story is one that can be easily retold and shared virally. Once you're telling those kinds of stories, your customers really will do the selling for you.

CHAPTER 13

COMPETE WITH INTENSITY

Who doesn't want to always beat the competition? Winning sales teams are maniacally focused on their competitors. Arrogance about your product compared to others on the market is not a winning strategy. Here's the attitude I suggest instead: Be humble, and "respect thy competition." It's a key function of the sales manager to help her team be aware and mindful of their competitors' strengths and weaknesses and to give the team a strategy for handling objections and asking the right eye-opening questions. You can't let your competitors plant *fear*, *uncertainty*, and *doubt* (FUD) in your customers' minds about your products and services; instead, you have to make sure that you and everyone on your team is competing with intensity.

The partnership between sales and marketing is critical to developing competitive sales strategies, tools, and culture. Work closely with your marketing partners to build a strong set of competitive tools that become differentiators for your sales team. Think back to the power of sales values and how you can empower a competitive spirit across your sales team. For example, one year at a sales kickoff, we decided to highlight the need for sales teams to be more aware of their competitors. The competitive landscape was heating up, and, like every company, we wanted to always win. As a way to magnify competitive strategies in deals, we created a mantra that became part of the sales culture: "Crush the competition." Every conversation, deal review, and sales tool had a competitive filter on it. We injected competitive intensity into our sales culture. We aligned sales and marketing to outmaneuver the competition. Armed with customer testimonials and videos, salespeople were inspired to crush the competition. I encourage you to look at your competitive market realities to come up with your own sales value related to crushing the competition; you can even give it a slogan, as we did, as long as it fits your culture.

The execution of competitive strategies begins with first-line sales managers and their sales teams. The hand-to-hand combat happens in executive conference rooms when salespeople meet their customers to learn more about their business. A well-informed discovery session is the primary weapon salespeople have to handle the land mines planted by their competitors. The battle continues in the follow-up emails reminding customers of their stated challenges and priorities, with links to videos and case studies.

Arrogance is the ultimate saboteur. Arrogance breeds happy ears—it makes you hear what you want to hear. Arrogance results in losing deals. I have learned so much from the thousands of sales professionals I've worked with over the years, including how to look at every competitive move in the context of a "strengths and weaknesses" framework. Understanding and respecting your competitors' strengths will help you handle objections with confidence. Humbly identifying competitive weaknesses will help you, consultatively, share value-based differentiators that are tied back to business challenges and priorities, helping you overcome land mines placed by your competitors. Focusing on value puts you in a consultative position rather than a defensive one. It's important to learn from your competitive sales wins, and it's even more important to learn from your losses. It seems counterintuitive to many, but spending time as a team dissecting a loss in a constructive way will actually improve your competence, confidence, and win rates.

Instilling an intense, competitive spirit in your team members and creating an unwavering focus on beating out competitors as part of your culture are important principles in sales management. It's up to you to make sure your team is living by former Intel CEO Andy Grove's mantra: "Only the paranoid survive."

LEARN FROM LOSSES

It takes courage to stand up and talk about the reasons why a deal was lost. After all, who wants to relive the pain? The reality is that salespeople learn from salespeople, and competitive losses are a very therapeutic way for salespeople to learn from each other. Competitive losses, as painful as they may be for that one salesperson, can be a huge inspiration for the rest of a sales team. Watch how popular competitive loss discussions are at sales-kickoff events and how much salespeople want to get the full story. Sales managers are in the perfect position to harness a constructive conversation around the lessons learned by team members who've lost a sale.

I have sat through many competitive-win and competitive-loss discussions. The sales managers who demonstrated true leadership started by creating a safe environment to share ideas. After experiencing a loss, one particular sales manager decided to bring the sales team together on a conference call. The salesperson was asked to come to the meeting prepared to do a play-by-play. There were no rehearsals and no one's words were scripted. The rawness of the conversation ultimately helped the entire team and ensured that the competitor would not get the upper hand again in future deals. The sales team listened and even brainstormed new ways to outmaneuver the competitor. They created a new competitive playbook that improved the team's success.

I watched a sales leader, Mark Wayland, with whom I have partnered with on many occasions, embrace the power of competitive-loss reviews. He hated losing, but he made sure to bring the team together to discuss what happened when he did. I remember on one occasion, he invited a few folks from headquarters to share in the competitive-loss discussion too. We learned so much about what was happening in the market. Our competitor had executed a new sales strategy. By taking the time to pause and review what had happened in this deal, everyone on the team benefited. The headquarters' folks learned, too, and in turn were able to create new competitive playbook tools to use proactively the next time one of our teams came up against this strategy again. The courage he demonstrated by sharing what happened in this loss helped many other sales teams. I'd like to report that some time after this loss review, this company came back and Mark's team was able to close the deal.

As you embark on your own competitive-loss discussions, give yourself a framework for a healthy dialogue. Have the call leader, whether it's a sales manager or an executive from marketing, be clear about the ground rules for the call. Start by having the salesperson, in a non-defensive way, share why they lost. It's good to have the salesperson unravel the deal by going through the sales process and telling the story. It's good to follow your sales process and include answers to questions about lead source, executive alignment, and solution fit. The salesperson should be honest and answer the question: Why didn't the customer choose them? The answer could be price, relationship, solution fit, or any other reason. Then shift the conversation to what could have been done differently. This is where the learning and a fruitful conversation can happen.

There is an additional side benefit of doing a competitive-loss analysis: Sometimes new information surfaces and the salesperson is able to think of an angle to reach back to their prospect with. Conduct these loss reviews with your team for each competitor as often as possible.

AUTOMATE COMPETITIVE SELLING STRATEGIES

As sales managers, you should also bring competitive intensity to life in team meetings, during coaching calls, and in one-on-ones. Make it one of your sales values and integrate with your sales system to proactively drive action. You can customize your sales system and capture competitors, competitive status, and competitive differentiators. The competitor field should have a list of all the competitors. When a salesperson selects a competitor's name in the drop-down value, something should happen, such as receiving an alert that includes links to the latest sales tools. This tactic represents a great example of how to blend intensity as a sales value with technology to ensure scale.

You can use automated workflow rules to push competitive tools, such as common objections and traps, to your salespeople when they encounter competitor strengths and weaknesses in real time. Imagine that a salesperson identifies a competitor by selecting them in the sales system, and that the technology then automates the dissemination of the latest competitive playbook, including objections and traps. That's fantastic information, right at your rep's fingertips!

Another great best practice is to have your reps assess how they're doing on a deal compared to the competition. You can have the system alert you when a salesperson indicates that he is behind the competition; you can then supply that rep with the resources he needs to close the deal.

BUILD A LIBRARY OF OBJECTIONS AND TRAPS

It goes without saying that your reps need to know their competitors, but building a powerful competitive-intelligence engine is not easy. The issue with competitive selling, especially in the high-technology world, is that the strategies employed by competitors are rapidly changing. A lot can be learned from the competitive strategies employed by sales teams and marketers in the high-technology sector. Using the same model of sharing lessons learned from a loss, bring sales teams together to brainstorm and role-play with each other their top objections and traps.

Start by focusing on one competitor at a time and begin a rigorous inventory of objections encountered in deals. Have each person on the sales team share as many objections as they can. Competitor strengths should be mapped to objections. Put yourself in your competitors' shoes and play out what they would say. Then share how you would counter. Run this exercise in person or virtually. It's a great way to bubble up all of the objections. Then as a team, begin dissecting why the objection is coming up in sales cycles, and create language to handle it. After creating a list of common objections and ways to handle them, have salespeople practice and personalize them. The words should be personalized to each salesperson's style. Remember, these objections are based on competitive strengths that are being communicated as objections by the customer. When these objections are prominent in your customer meetings, take note that your competitor is outselling you.

One of the most common objections that come up with companies occurs when a customer says, "Your competitor is good enough, and they are less expensive." When that happens, focus on the existing relationship and what you learned in discovery. Dust off the value-creation calculators. Then, be ready to go on the offensive and create a winning competitive strategy.

The second half of the competitive exercise is to switch over to competitive weaknesses and turn the weaknesses into questions or traps that could be asked. When handling objections, use value-based facts. Respect your competition; don't bash, and don't be defensive. Come across as consultative. Explain the trade-offs in the context of their business challenges and desired outcomes. Quantify the value of their weaknesses. Map your solution strengths to weaknesses. Use questions and pose them as benefits. Ask questions that make your customers really wonder if they are making the right choice.

BE PROACTIVE WITH COMPETITIVE-DEAL WAR ROOMS

There are a number of ways to be proactive in deals and to avoid being outsold by the competition. Start by identifying all the deals that are lagging behind a competitor. If you are capturing this information in your sales system, it will be easy to run a report; otherwise you'll need to reach out to your team to tap into this list.

Once these deals are identified, rally sales-support resources to help diagnose why each may be behind the competition. Schedule a sales huddle, or as some call it a competitive "war room," call for each deal; in this call, the team will come together in a form of deal therapy. The sales teams are offered a chance to share how things are going. Rally executives, product managers, and other resources to help the team be successful. Make sure all members of the sales team feel comfortable requesting these war-room calls on their own, too.

Having executed thousands of competitive war rooms over the years at salesforce.com, I can attest to their power. We created a competitive hotline or deal therapy for sales teams. Here is how it worked. A salesperson would self-select that they needed help by opting in for a competitive war-room call, or they'd mark their competitive status behind competition. The net effect was the same. We would swarm the deal with expert resources to diagnose the deal strategy and get back ahead of competition. The power of the competitive war rooms spread virally and became a big part of the culture at salesforce.com and the hundreds of companies with whom we shared this sales process best practice. Salespeople appreciate knowing that help is available upon request. Use your sales process to guide you. Dive into what you know—and what you don't know—about the deal and about executive relationships. Get clarity on why the team thinks they are behind the competition, and begin to build a strategy for outplaying your competitors.

MEASURE WINS AND LOSSES IN TERRITORY

One of the most successful sales managers I know shared his team's sales reports and dashboards with me a few years back. The interaction stuck with me. Besides the regular pipeline and revenue reporting, I was shown a level of competitive intensity that defines how he expected his team to perform. He was living Andy Grove's mantra of "only the paranoid survive." His reports highlighted deals closing by month, by quarter, and by year, showing which were ahead of and behind the competition. His reports were filtered by competitor name. He referenced these reports in every team meeting. He uses the report and the conclusions drawn from it to prioritize activity and coaching conversations. For example, if a certain competitor starts coming up more and more in deals, this sales leader is able to identify this trend very early on and act on it. A competitive sales huddle is scheduled with the team and expert resources from headquarters. He encourages his team to share their experiences, both strengths and weaknesses, in a bid to refresh the competitive objections and traps. His management style represents how important it is to use data to drive action.

• • •

Igniting competitive spirit in your sales campaigns is not a one-time activity. It should be part of every sales step and activity. It emerges in prospecting and deal strategies and is a big consideration in account planning too. Knowing competitors during discovery ultimately helps shape how critical business issues become a solution. The solution is informed by obstacles and is riddled with land mines that are used to differentiate. Presentations, business cases, and proposals are filled with competitive strategies. The best salespeople are thinking about their competitors in every email, conversation, and moment of every sales cycle. Winning salespeople are always *maniacally* focused on their competitors' position and next move. Live the mantra—crush the competition.

CHAPTER 14

GROW STRATEGIC ACCOUNTS

I firmly believe that investing time in building relationships and developing account strategies is time well spent, especially when you're doing it with the right accounts, the right mind-set, and the right team. Account planning isn't something you need to do with every account you're selling to or in every segment; for example, it's unlikely that you'll drive a strategic account-planning program in your small business segments with every one of your small business customers. On the bigger accounts, though, this is a mandatory practice that is expected by fellow team members and deal contributors, too. For the most part, sales executives do account planning opportunistically rather than being proactive. As the CEO of your territory, it's up to you to help your sales teams prioritize their time—and that includes helping them decide which accounts to develop a strategic plan for and helping them do it well. The words in this chapter are inspired by the thousands of hours of account-planning sessions we lead. Also, many of the principles are guided (and validated) by years of best practices nurtured by Donal Daly and his team.[27]

The road to strategic, long-term relationships with customers starts with a well-thought-out plan created by a team of people and ultimately validated by a customer. Some of the best salespeople I've worked with had such great relationships with their executive buyers that they invited the customer to actually participate in the account-planning process. Who doesn't want their customer to validate an account strategy? I remember on one account I worked with, the customer thought that our strategies were not aggressive enough and wanted to see them implemented sooner. You can bet that we took his input seriously and changed our plan.

You want your team's account plans to be aligned with your customers' top priorities and to represent a deep understanding of the customer's business. Everyone knows that you have to have an account plan for strategic accounts. More often than not, strategic account planning ends up becoming a secondary or annual sales activity rather than a primary activity and one that is ongoing. The plan's ultimate goal is to align a team around a core set of goals and actions to drive revenue.

Everyone has heard about account planning as a sales skill and a management coaching tool, but most have not heard salespeople say it has changed their careers. In this chapter, you'll learn or refresh your skills around coaching your teams to think strategically about their accounts. You'll understand your role in account planning and the immense value you can add to your sales teams. This chapter is about the shift in perspective you'll want to instill in your sales culture. I remember Frank van Veenendaal sitting down with me at the beginning of our journey and saying, "Solve the behaviors first, then solve the technology." Strategic account planning is a way of thinking, and when it becomes part of a sales team's rhythm, it can result in business outcomes that far exceed expectations.

IT STARTS WITH YOU

Effective account planning starts with you. When it comes to being strategic about selling to key accounts, you need to lead by example and be clear about your expectations for the team. As a sales manager, you must be the loudest proponent of strategic account planning, and your actions must speak for themselves. Empower your sales teams to host strategy sessions for their key accounts. Attend them and be an active participant. Facilitate best practice sharing and brainstorming. Make these meetings count. Have them publish agendas and provide them with the support they need to make sure their account goals and these strategic conversations are happening.

I once came to an account-planning session ready to talk strategy. Within ten minutes of the scheduled ninety-minute account-planning session, the sales manager started diving into the forecast and talking about a specific opportunity for that account. Rather than being strategic about it, he was being pre-scriptive and too specific; he had converted the account-planning strategy session into a deal review. The mood of the room sank, and there was nothing anyone could do. Everyone started looking at their devices while the sales manager and salesperson had a one-on-one deal discussion that should not have happened the way it did. No one was empowered to stand up and remind the sales manager what the goal of the meeting was. It was tough to argue because of the size of the deal and the importance of the transaction to the success of the quarter, so the session stayed offtrack until it ended. I learned a lot about making sure expectations and ground rules are set before these kinds of meetings.

The negative impact on team motivation was considerable. The sales manager lost credibility, and the salesperson became discouraged and demotivated. I'm sure there were many reasons why this salesperson eventually quit, but I know that this experience was a deciding factor—he told me so himself! This salesperson wanted a strategic, consultative sales job, and if the sales manager didn't help make that happen, then why work on the team? The other people in the room, from other teams around the company, were also frustrated; they had signed up to help grow this account, and they felt that their time was not well spent. In the end, everyone walked away with a warped perspective of what strategic selling was.

If you find yourself having the urge to move from strategy to tactics in meetings and workshops that are explicitly about strategic account planning, resist the urge, lest your team also end up like this one. Instead, encourage everyone to participate in the strategy discussion; in an ideal world, your salespeople will stand up and be the ultimate facilitators. They'll be able to drive a room of executives through brainstorming and sharing ideas. They'll be able to listen more than talk and let the creative process happen. If your salespeople are able to do this, then that's great. If they aren't there yet, though, then it's your job to step in and mentor.

START WITH A BEGINNER'S MIND

As the team coach, you want to inspire the creative process around developing account strategies that will result in huge customer value and mega-deals. The Zen Buddhist concept of the "beginner's mind" is something everyone should pick up before they begin diving into the creative side of sales strategy and account planning. The saying goes, "In the beginner's mind there are many possibilities; in the expert's mind there are few." This is such a great concept for taking a fresh look at a familiar situation. Suggest to each new salesperson you hire and anyone wanting to kick-start their creative juices that he or she read *Zen Mind, Beginner's Mind* by Shunryu Suzuki.

The notion of a "beginner's mind" also helps a team get out of a rut on an account that may have had zero revenue growth. Account teams sometimes continue to focus on the same strategies, the same executives, and the same value propositions with their accounts. You can use the "beginner's mind" philosophy to shake the proverbial tree with some of your accounts.

A winning sales culture uses account planning to think bigger. I've participated in some very painful sessions where sales managers expect the sales team to come to the table with a completed account plan and strategy, undermining the intended collaborative process involving creativity and brainstorming. Take a moment and consider how much of a shift this framing can have on the motivation of a team. It might take a bit longer to get a strategy going on a specific account. However, once the strategy is identified, the extended sales team will be aligned and ready to go to battle together.

MAKE ACCOUNT PLANNING PART OF THE TEAM'S DNA

Take your sales team with you on a journey to be more strategic about their accounts. I have worked with some sales managers who have shown me how to get teams to embrace strategic account planning. I had the pleasure of learning from some of the world's best. In order to create the best of the best, I amalgamated a set of account-planning experiences of different sales managers into one super sales manager.

It all starts with setting goals for your teams. It's unrealistic to think that each salesperson will be able to drive strategic account planning in every account. Be realistic about time and resource commitments. Set a workable number of tier 1 accounts for each salesperson—one is optimal and ten is too many. Remember, the goal is to be strategic, and loading up your best salespeople with all the strategic accounts and having them drive many account strategies at once will not serve your business goals—or theirs. Be clear on what you expect from your teams in terms of time commitment and output per month.

I have heard salespeople say that they want fewer accounts so that they can focus, be strategic, and build more value for their customers and ultimately for their families. On several occasions, I have seen experienced salespeople approach me or their sales managers and ask for fewer accounts. One of these reps ended up closing a nine-digit transaction after dropping the number of strategic accounts from five to one.

Have a launch call or meeting with your sales team to focus on strategic account planning. Explain the benefits. Share examples from your current company or previous experiences. Monetize the value of account planning. Highlight the strategic accounts and make them the most visible to the team.

I had the good fortune of witnessing first-hand several of these kickoff calls, and I was in awe of the sales managers who hosted them. They were inspirational. They took matters into their own hands, creating a theme and energy around a program that might otherwise be considered an administrative chore. One sales leader running a large organization used a superheroes theme and came up with a brand for these strategic accounts. He called his strategic account list the "super sixty" to inspire super action. He then added in a bit of the competitive spirit by creating a dashboard of activity, pipeline generated, and closed business resulting from these "super sixty" accounts. His program was the talk of the sales organization, and the results were astounding, too.

EMBRACE A PROCESS AND KEEP IT SIMPLE

There are many different processes out there to help align your sales teams and shape the right behaviors. While all the account-planning methodologies vary a bit, fundamentally they are grounded in similar principles. Regardless of which account-planning process works for you, remember to keep it simple and be consistent. Focus on building a strategy and a clear set of action items to execute on with your team. Use an action plan to empower your salespeople to keep the momentum going and everyone engaged. Accountability is critical to success.

Here is an account-planning process that has worked for many sales teams I personally worked with over the years.

Do Research

Follow your sales research best practice principles. Make sure you are clear on expectations for the research your salespeople should be doing on their accounts. There might be some unique best practices that have emerged as critical to developing an account strategy with other accounts at your company. For example, when I was selling the Partner Relationship Management solution, we would do an audit of a prospect's partners as part of the account-planning process to uncover what was working and what was not working. One sales manager I know published to the team a one-page set of questions simply titled "Things You Should Know About Your Accounts."

Build Department or Business-Unit Analysis Maps

One of the most valuable exercises I was introduced to was one where, for any given account, you identify what you know and what you don't know. I love doing this exercise. The best sales managers

set the expectation with their teams when coming to the table for a
"what you know and don't know" brainstorm session that it's okay
not to have all the answers. How empowering! They would use
language like, "Let's figure it out together."

For this exercise, we would find a big whiteboard or use technology to capture the information in real time. List out the divisions and departments, and then start marking what you know and
what you don't know about each one. We would structure the conversation around a common set of dimensions. I had fun doing this
on every continent with sales teams that came from different companies and cultures; it worked everywhere. The simplicity of this
analysis always resulted in a clear sense of where the opportunity
was. As a sales manager, it's your job to empower similar collaboration and analysis across your strategic accounts.

Some of the dimensions of the business-unit or department
analysis include number of employees, revenues, profitability,
growth trends, top executive, last contact with the top executive,
executive top priorities, and top corporate initiatives.

The intent here isn't to provide an exhaustive list but to provide you with a framework to structure a conversation that will get
your teams to think more strategically about the value they can
provide their customers.

Create an Account-Based Strategy

Use the analysis conducted in the business-unit "whiteboarding"
brainstorm session to build an account strategy that the entire team
is excited about. Focus on areas where there is great alignment
between pain and solution impact. I remember sitting through
one of these where at the end, the team agreed that there were
a number of divisions we would not go after at this time, because
our solution was not a good fit. It's great to reach these account-
strategy realizations earlier rather than later.

Build a Political Influence Map

A critical part of every account plan is the organizational influence map. Know where power is. Know who are your "friends" and who are not. Visualize and create the political map of the buyer's organization. Identify the right people, gain access, and develop support to give you a competitive advantage to win. Create executive profiles that include buyer roles like decision maker, evaluator, approver, influencer, and business user. Identify their status whether they are a supporter, mentor, neutral, nonsupporter, or enemy. It's important to know who your friends are.

Create a Team-Based Action List

Without action there are no results. I have seen many teams develop and assemble amazing account strategies but miss capturing the necessary actions—the to-do list. Everyone on the extended team has come together for a reason. They want to help the salesperson build customer value and close a big deal. Keep a running list of action items during the meeting, and then review them at the end. Assign owners, and remember: The salesperson shouldn't own all the actions. The salesperson's job is to drive the strategy, owning some of the actions but mainly quarterbacking the activity and the deal. I always appreciated the salespeople who sent out the action items in a follow-up note after the meeting and then sent me reminders. They might have thought they were being a bit of a pain, but the reality is we're all busy, and we need someone to keep the momentum going. That's the job of the salesperson. This is a great coaching opportunity for sales managers.

Meet Regularly as a Team

Make sure everyone walks away with a clear set of expectations around goals, actions, and deliverable dates. Set a regular cadence for meeting. Have a team check-in meeting at a frequency that is acceptable to the team. Keep these check-in meetings very focused and action oriented. Don't try to do everything in one meeting. Instead, setting up more frequent meetings will increase account-ability and results.

Convert Strategies into Qualified Opportunities

As the strategies are put into action, nurture a culture that holds people accountable. Ask the tough questions when the sales team comes together. Once the executive interactions and conversations happen and pain is identified and validated, shift the focus to managing an opportunity. There is a point, once an opportunity is identified and qualified, when the actions created from your account-strategy work shift to sales process work. Be there to keep the teams honest, and celebrate their successes broadly. These kinds of accomplishments are also great motivators for the team to create their own qualified opportunities by being strategic with their accounts.

Revise Account Strategy

Remind the teams that iteration and agility are principles that pay good dividends. Don't fear changes in account strategy when new information is discovered. Be agile and be open to an account strategy that evolves with market conditions, mergers and acquisitions, and organizational changes inside your accounts.

BE PROUD OF YOUR TEAM'S WORK AND SHARE IT

I experienced an interesting phenomenon: Sales managers would send me their sales teams' best account plans to review, and while they wanted me to help with the account, what they were really doing was showcasing their teams' great work. I admired these sales managers who were truly proud of what their teams accomplished. An account plan is a great deliverable that represents the best thinking of an account; why not share it?

Account plans are used to brief executives, and in some cases they are also shared with customers themselves. Be thoughtful. Be strategic. Be transparent.

When you tell your teams that you'll be sharing the best account plans with senior executives at your company, you're sure to get even more great work from them.

• • •

Strategic account planning should be recognized as a differentiator and value creator, not an administrative chore completed once a year. Make it be part of the rhythm of your business. Engage a broader team to brainstorm new account strategies. Keep the team accountable with the strategies and actions created in the planning sessions. It's up to you, the sales manager, to make strategic account planning an important part of your team's culture and pipeline generation strategy.

PARTING ADVICE

At this point, you are not only thinking like a CEO and acting like an entrepreneur, you're also already using the best practices and stories from this book in your business. Your sales teams are inspired and performing like the rock stars they deserve to be. As a sales manager, you're empowered to build your business. It starts with you and your entrepreneurial spirit. I once ran a global sales event themed "The Power of You," and that theme is true here, too.

Your sales team is your best asset. Start by building or embracing sales values that will drive the culture and cadence needed to inspire the right set of actions on your teams. Nurture a culture of winning as a team and never losing alone. Help your sales teams understand the power of their internal and external networks. Make every moment a learning and coaching moment for your teams, and embrace the new modes of social and mobile delivery of sales training. Integrate learning and best practice sharing with the rhythm of your business by making them a part of your weekly team meetings. Have a plan that maps to your business goals and is personalized for each and every person on your teams. Be thoughtful about your communications, and remember that every word counts. Motivate your teams to be the best they can be. Make onboarding a team activity for you and your team to improve ramp time, powered by accountability and peer-to-peer mentoring.

Creating a sales playbook based on your selling culture and best practices will energize your sales process. Bring your sales process to life by integrating it with your weekly team meetings, deal reviews, and customer-engagement strategies. Be customer focused and map your sales process to your customer's buying process. Make prospecting a top priority for every salesperson on your team by coaching him or her to block time out each week for this important business-building activity. Make prospecting and pipeline generation a team activity with shared goals and best practice sharing around outreach strategies. Instill a culture of curiosity-based selling, starting with thoughtful discovery to solve big problems. Uncover and quantify your customers' top business issues and corporate initiatives so that you and your team become trusted value-add consultants. Drive action with transformational and emotional customer stories that build trust. Always be paranoid about your competition, and make sure you are being honest with yourself about your relative competitive position.

There are some specific words of advice I'd like to share with you to help you tie together all these themes into a cohesive sales-productivity strategy. You can't do it alone. Partner with marketing, sales operations, and IT early and often. Be agile, and don't be afraid to iterate your business, team, and sales-campaign strategies.

PARTNER WITH MARKETING AND IT

In my tenure at salesforce.com, besides partnering with sales leaders to propel sales productivity, I also had a strong partnership with marketing and IT; I knew we needed each other. On the marketing side, my team and I formed a great working relationship with the CMO and all of the product marketing and field-marketing leaders. It helped us execute, and, more important, it kept us aligned. Winning sales managers also adopted a similar organizational philosophy.

The sales managers who were always on stage at kickoff and on the top of the sales leaderboards were the ones who invited marketing to their team meetings and made sure their teams were on message. These sales managers were using the latest sales tools and appreciated how marketing resources and tools were deployed to build pipeline and accelerate deals. These sales managers were also not shy about sharing what was working and what wasn't working. These winning sales managers let marketing and sales operations enable but also observe so that they could create even better tools.

IT is your friend. Engage them early and often. Work within the boundaries of your corporate IT policies while you're finding creative ways to drive more value to your customers. When IT is looking for volunteers to pilot a project, if you can handle it, do it. You never know when you'll need a favor, and it's always good to have friends in IT.

• • •

As I reflect on my days in my dad's furniture store or cutting lawns or selling financial services or selling enterprise software, all the way up to leading sales productivity at salesforce.com, I'm humbled by the amazing partnerships (and friends) I made along the way. I've been deeply privileged to be in a position to learn from "the best of the best." Not only that, but I've had the amazing opportunity to create amazing value for customers and sales teams. A good friend and mentor of mine once said to me in our early San Francisco start-up days: "Elay, did you move the company forward today? Did you make a positive influence in someone's life?" I've taken this question with me and have asked myself this every day in my professional career. I have worked with and mentored sales teams made up of motivated, professional, competitive people who were driven to learn, driven to win, and driven to innovate. I have always been passionate about helping salespeople be the best they can be. I hope this book inspires you the way my friends and mentors have inspired me.

There is a revolution happening. First-line sales managers and salespeople are at the epicenter of it. As in the days of Plato and Socrates, when people would come together and share their experiences and learn from each other, the sales world is poised to come together to build a strong global sales community. It starts with you and your team, and then it spreads team by team. The most amazing successes and personal growth I've witnessed in my career have been built around salespeople coming together as a team, creating communities of effort with other stakeholders—including their best customers—and sharing with each other in order to become the best they can be. I am absolutely convinced because I've seen how community sharing bears the fruits of productivity gains. Embrace SalesHood as a state of sharing real-life sales experiences and as a commitment to learn and teach best practices.

In closing, let me invite you to experience the exhilaration of becoming the CEO of your territory and business. You, the sales manager, are in the ideal position to foster the climate of Sales-Hood in which everyone wins: you, your sales team, your company, and your customers.

ACKNOWLEDGMENTS

There are many people to thank and recognize for providing me with amazing support, mentorship, and friendship while I created and lived SalesHood. I want to thank my wife for all the hours, days, months, and years I spent writing (and rewriting) this book. I could not have done it without you. Thank you to my kids for motivating me to be the best I can be. And I want to recognize my sisters for their unconditional love and for always reminding me who I am.

I want to recognize the thousands of salespeople, sales engineers, and sales managers that I worked with, sold with, or trained at sales-force.com. You inspired me to sit down, share our story, and write this book. Our collective sales experience is the inspiration for this book. Thank you for being such amazing professionals and inspiring me to nurture a winning sales culture.

I want to thank my dear friends Ron Tattum, Andrew O'Driscoll, David Krigstin, Jake Hofwegen, Eric Hills, and Steve Rubenfaer for life-long friendships and advice shared with me over decades of great times together. Thanks for always being such pillars of strength in my life. I'm also very fortunate to have been introduced to Arthur Do, my cofounder, partner, and friend.

I want to thank Frank van Veenendaal for the opportunity to create and lead the global sales productivity team at salesforce.com. Your mentorship and direction enabled us to stay focused on the most critical priorities. I also appreciate all the advice and guidance you gave me with this book too. I would like to thank Linda Crawford, who was my boss, during the amazing "sales productivity" years. Thank you for the hours and hours of strategy and planning sessions we had on boot camps, sales training, certifications, kickoffs, and so much more. Also, thank you for the support on SalesHood—the book and the company. Thank you Brian Millham for being such a great partner and friend. I always knew your office door was open to me. Many of the programs discussed in this book we ran together. Thank you, Jim Steele, for being such a great advocate of the work I did and being a great mentor to me during my time at salesforce.com and after I left. You are all amazing professionals (and friends) and I look forward to working with all of you again one day soon. Also, thank you Marc Benioff for your leadership and vision.

Thank you Barry Rhein and Donal Daly for welcoming me into your professional and personal lives. You partnered and brainstormed with me many times, creating the foundation for this book and our new Sales-Hood venture. Thank you for being such great friends and advisers to me.

I want to thank the amazing productivity leaders that worked with me at salesforce.com to create the sales productivity program. I'd like to give a special thank-you to Renny Monaghan, Dennis Jeske, Theresa Ludvigson, Amy Regan Morehouse, Jared Litwin, Mike Milburn, Kardyhm Kelly, Julie Hibson, and Josh Aranoff. We accomplished so much together and I learned so much from each of you. Your dedication and passion enabled us to create the most productive sales productivity machine in the industry.

The SalesHood concept was enriched by collaborating with Tom Banahan, Brent Chudoba, JD Cain, Scott Johnson, Maureen Kelly,

Steven Schneider, Mike Prowak, Brian Martin, Jeff Honeycomb, Benjamin Swanson, AJ Stahl, Corinne Sklar, Mike Minnelli, Kurt Foeller, Tim Leads, Michael Gear, Aaron Hierholzer, Tom Strachan, Tim McManus, Brian Louie, Genevieve Astrelli-Godson, Kurt Shaver, Ken Leeder, Chris Do, Matt Holleran, Scott Crawford, and many salespeople who supported and joined us in the early days of the SalesHood venture.

Will Moxley, Adi Kuruganti, Matt Morris, Ryan Davis, Woodson Martin, and Amy Regan Morehouse (again), thanks for making PRM a reality. PRM rocks! We created something special that revolutionized the way companies think of channels of distribution. It was PRM that was the stepping-stone at salesforce.com for each of us.

There are a number of sales and marketing professionals who I am forever grateful to for always being available on speed dial. I appreciate all of the brainstorming, ideation, and conversations. Thank you, Lindsey Armstrong, Dan Dal Degan, Mike Pliner, Valerie Wolloch, Kevin Egan, Dave Rudnitsky, Gordon Gower, Hilarie Koplow-McAdams, Craig Shull, Dominic Dinardo, Dave Burkhardt, Mark Wayland, Polly Sumner, Mark Morrissey, Susan St. Ledger, Wendy Reed, Eric Eyken-Sluyters, and Hal Libben, who passed away way before his time. And a special thanks to Kraig Swensrud for our amazing partnership. We proved that when marketing and sales are aligned, amazing things do happen. Thank you, my friends.

I would like to take a moment to remember a dear friend, Peter Fishchel, for always being there with a big-brotherly smile and embrace. Your face is always in my mind, my friend.

A special note to my extended family of uncles, aunts, and cousins spread around the world from all sides of my family whom I appreciate and my grandparents Regina, Issac, Lucie, and Elie

I'd like to end this part of the book by thanking my parents, Etty and Maurice, for giving me the love, support, and opportunities to become the person I am. You gave me so much and I'm forever grateful. Shalom!

NOTES

PREFACE

1   *Wiktionary*, s.v. "Selfhood," last modified June 18, 2013, http:// en.wiktionary.org/wiki/selfhood.

CHAPTER 1

2   Benjamin Barber, *If Mayors Ruled the World* (New Haven: Yale University Press, 2013).

3   Thomas Friedman, "I Want to Be a Mayor," *New York Times*, July 27, 2013.

4   Jennifer Bradley and Bruce Katz, *The Metropolitan Revolution: How Cities and Metros Are Fixing Our Broken Politics and Fragile Economy* (Washington, DC: The Brookings Institution, 2013).

5   I attended Date with Destiny in 2013 as a personal guest of Tony Robbins and Walter Rogers and appreciated so much the power of visualizing a future as a way to empower performance.

CHAPTER 2

6   Yukari Iwatani Kane and Ian Sherr, "Secrets From Apple's Genius Bar: Full Loyalty, No Negativity," *Wall Street Journal*, June 15, 2011, http://online.wsj.com/article/SB10001424052702304563104576364071955678908.html.

7   Marc Benioff, *Behind the Cloud* (Hoboken, NJ: Jossey-Bass, 2009).

8   Find the Dreamforce YouTube channel at http://www.youtube.com/user/dreamforce.

CHAPTER 3

9   Brent Adamson, Matthew Dixon, and Nicholas Toman, "Dismantling the Sales Machine," *Harvard Business Review*, November 2013.

10 Henry Mintzberg, "Rebuilding Companies as Communities," *Harvard Business Review*, July 2009.

CHAPTER 4

11 Suzanne Fogel, David Hoffmeister, Richard Rocco, and Daniel P. Strunk, "Teaching Sales," *Harvard Business Review*, July–August 2012.

12 "Kevin Spacey Urges TV Channels to Give Control to Viewers," YouTube video, from a speech at the Edinburgh International Television Festival, recorded and posted by the *Telegraph* (UK), August 23, 2013, http://www.youtube.com/watch?v=P0ukYf_xvgc.

13 "How Web Video Powers Global Innovation," a TED Talks video from Chris Anderson at TED Global 2010, filmed in July 2010 and posted September 2010, http://www.ted.com/talks/chris_anderson_how_web_video_powers_global_innovation.html.

14 Definition written by Donal Daly, CEO of the TAS Group.

CHAPTER 5

15 There are many different numbers floating around from many different training companies and consultancies. I calculated the number of days every year while I was at salesforce.com.

CHAPTER 6

16 "The Clues to a Great Story," a TED Talks video of a speech by Andrew Stanton at the TED 2012 conference, filmed in February 2012 and posted March 2012, http://www.ted.com/talks/andrew_stanton_the_clues_to_a _great_story.html.

17 S. Anthony Iannarino, "10 Questions to Start Your Week," *The Sales Blog*, July 21, 2013, http://thesalesblog.com/blog/2013/07/21/10-questions-to-start-your-week/.

CHAPTER 7

18 Gabe Zichermann, *Gamification* (website), http://www.gamification.co /gabe-zichermann/.

19 Tadhg Kelly, "Everything You'll Ever Need to Know About Gamification," *TechCrunch* (blog), November 17, 2012, http://techcrunch.com/2012/11/17 /everything-youll-ever-need-to-know-about-gamification/.

20 Milton Moskowitz and Charles Kapelke, "25 Top-Paying Companies," *CNN Money*, last updated January 26, 2011, http://money.cnn.com/galleries/2011/pf/jobs/1101/gallery.best_companies_top_paying.fortune/index .html.

21 The discussion of vision and metrics is based on the V2MOM—vision, values, methods, obstacles, and metrics—created by Marc Benioff at sales force.com.

22 Salesforce.com mission statement, http://www.salesforcefoundation.org /mission.

CHAPTER 11

23 You can learn more about Barry Rhein's methodology at SellingThrough Curiosity.com.

24 Thank you to my friend Shirzad Chamine for connecting the world of anthropology to the world of sales. He introduces the phrase *fascinated anthropologist* in his book *Positive Intelligence*.

25 Back in 1999, when I worked at Allegis Corporation, Hal Libben, Mark Morrissey, and Dennis Ryan introduced me to the notion of a shared vision in the sales process. I have never forgotten it.

CHAPTER 12

26 Michael Bosworth and Ben Zoldan, *What Great Salespeople Do* (New York: McGraw-Hill, 2012).

CHAPTER 14

27 Donal Daly, *Account Planning in Salesforce* (Cork, Ireland: Oak Tree Press, 2013).

INDEX

ABOUT THE AUTHOR

Elay Cohen is a Silicon Valley technology executive and entrepreneur. He is the cofounder and CEO of SalesHood, a "software as a service" cloud platform and online community for sales professionals. Previous to SalesHood, Elay was the Senior Vice President for Sales Productivity at salesforce.com. He was recognized as the company's "top executive of the year" in 2011. At salesforce.com, Elay created the sales enablement practice, leading the teams that executed sales training, onboarding, and deal support for thousands of sales executives. Elay also created the Partner Relationship Management market and product category for salesforce.com. Elay lives with his family in San Francisco, California.